TWO NOBLE LIVES

Two Noble Lives

*John Wycliffe and
Martin Luther*

by
David J Deane

JOHN RITCHIE LTD
CHRISTIAN PUBLICATIONS

40 Beansburn, Kilmarnock, Scotland

ISBN-13: 978 1 907731 80 8

Copyright © 2013 by John Ritchie Ltd.
40 Beansburn, Kilmarnock, Scotland

www.ritchiechristianmedia.co.uk

All rights reserved. No part of this publication may be reproduced, stored in a retrievable system, or transmitted in any form or by any other means – electronic, mechanical, photocopy, recording or otherwise – without prior permission of the copyright owner.

Typeset by John Ritchie Ltd., Kilmarnock
Printed by Bell & Bain Ltd., Glasgow

JOHN WICLIFFE

THE

MORNING STAR OF THE REFORMATION

CONTENTS.

CHAP.		PAGE
I.	PAPAL ENGLAND,	9
II.	EARLY YEARS AND COLLEGE LIFE,	17
III.	THE POPE OR THE KING,	27
IV.	WICLIFFE'S BATTLE WITH THE MENDICANT FRIARS,	35
V.	WICLIFFE APPOINTED A ROYAL COMMISSIONER,	44
VI.	PERSECUTION,	52
VII.	THE ENGLISH BIBLE,	70
VIII.	TRANSUBSTANTIATION,	84
IX.	CONCLUSION,	95

JOHN WICLIFFE.

CHAPTER I.

Papal England.

'We wait for light, but behold obscurity; for brightness, but we walk in darkness."—ISA. lix. 9.

IN the Middle Ages amidst the nations of Europe, two powers contended for supremacy—the Pope and the King. The Pope, as the Vicar of Jesus Christ, first assumed the title of Universal Bishop, and afterwards claimed temporal dominion over all the monarchs of Christendom. Long and fierce struggles ensued in consequence of this claim, and much blood was shed. In some countries the strife was carried on for centuries, but in England it was happily terminated at an early period. The great man to whose wisdom, patriotism, and piety the nation mainly owes this happy result, was John Wicliffe.

In the early years of the thirteenth century, the kingdom of England became subject to the Pope. A dispute had arisen between King John and the canons of Canterbury concerning the election of an archbishop for that diocese, in place of Hubert, who died in 1205. Both the canons and the king appealed to the Pope, and sent agents to Rome. The pontifical chair was then filled by Innocent III., who, like his predecessor, Gregory VII., was vigorously striving to subordinate the rights and powers of princes to the Papal See, and to take into his own hands all the ecclesiastical appointments of the Christian nations, so that through the bishops and priests he might govern at his will all the kingdoms of Europe.

Innocent annulled both the election of the canons and also that of the king, and caused his own nominee, Cardinal Langton, to be chosen to the see of Canterbury. But, more than this, he claimed the right for the Pontiff of appointing to this seat of dignity for all coming time.

John was enraged when he saw this action taken by the Pope. If he now appoints to the see of Canterbury, the most important dignity in England save the throne, will he not also appoint to the throne itself? The king protested with many oaths that the papal nominee should never sit in the archiepiscopal chair. He turned the canons of Canterbury out of doors, ordered all the prelates and abbots to leave the kingdom, and bade defiance to Rome. Innocent III.

smote England with interdict. The church-doors were closed, the lights at the altars were extinguished, the bells ceased to be rung, the crosses and images were taken down and laid on the ground, infants were baptised in the church-porch, marriages were celebrated in the churchyard, the dead were buried in ditches or in the open fields. No one durst rejoice, or eat flesh, or shave his beard, or pay any decent attention to his person or apparel. It was meet that only signs of distress, mourning, and woe should be visible throughout a land over which there rested the wrath of the Almighty; for so did the men of those days account the ban of the Pontiff.

King John braved this state of things for two years, when Innocent pronounced sentence of excommunication upon him; absolving his subjects from their allegiance, and offering the crown of England to Philip Augustus, King of France. Philip collected a mighty armament, and prepared to cross the Channel and invade the territories of the excommunicated king.

At this time John was on bad terms with his barons on account of his many vices, and dared not depend upon their support. He saw the danger in which he stood, and, losing what little courage he possessed, determined upon an unconditional surrender to the Pope. He claimed an interview with Pandolf, the papal legate, and, after a short conference, engaged to make full restitution to the clergy for the losses they had suffered. He then "resigned England and Ireland to God, to St. Peter and St.

Paul, and to Pope Innocent and his successors in the apostolic chair, agreeing to hold these dominions as feudatory of the Church of Rome, by the annual payment of a thousand marks; also stipulating that if he or his successors should ever presume to infringe this charter, they should instantly, except upon admonition they repented of their offence, forfeit all right to their dominions."

The transaction was ended by the King of England kneeling before the legate of the Pope, and, taking the crown from his head, offering it to Pandolf, saying, "Here I resign the crown of the realm of England into the Pope's hand, Innocent III., and put me wholly in his mercy and ordinance."

This event occurred on the 15th May, 1213; and never has there been a moment of profounder humiliation for England.

This dastardly conduct on the part of their king aroused the patriotism of the nation. The barons determined that they would never be the slaves of a Pope, and, unsheathing their swords, they vowed to maintain the ancient liberties of England or die in the attempt. On the 15th of June, 1215, they compelled John to sign Magna Charta at Runnymede, and thus in effect to tell Innocent that he revoked his vow of vassalage, and took back the kingdom which he had laid at his feet. The Pope was furious. He issued a bull declaring that he annulled the charter, and proclaiming all its obligations and guarantees void.

From this reign England may date her love of

liberty and dread of popery. At its commencement, the distinction which had existed since the conquest between Norman and Saxon was broadly marked, and the Norman baron looked upon his Saxon neighbour with contempt, his common form of indignant denial being, "Do you take me for an Englishman?" Towards its close there was a drawing together of the two races, and from their amalgamation was afterwards formed the bold and strong English people, who, in the fourteenth century, offered so stout a resistance to the arrogant claims of the Roman See.

But, while feeling a dread of the papacy, the people still held to the doctrines of Rome. Enveloped in ignorance and sunk in social degradation and vice, they had not the Scriptures to enlighten their path. The Bible was a sealed book. Freedom of conscience was denied, and the religion of the country consisted in outward ceremonials, appealing to the senses but not influencing the heart. D'Aubigné, the historian of the Reformation, states, "Magnificent churches and the marvels of religious art, with ceremonies and a multitude of prayers and chantings, dazzled the eyes, charmed the ears, and captivated the senses, but testified also to the absence of every strong moral and Christian disposition, and the predominance of worldliness in the Church. At the same time, the adoration of images and relics, saints, angels, and Mary, the mother of God, transporting the real Mediator from the throne of mercy to the seat of vengeance, at once indicated and kept up among the people that ignorance of truth and absence of grace which characterise popery."

Foxe, the martyrologist, quaintly says, " The people were taught to worship no other thing but that which they did see; and they did see almost nothing which they did not worship."

The nation groaned under the encroachments and exactions of the Pontiff. Not content with the ancient patrimony of Peter's pence, the Pope strove in various ways to drain the country of its wealth. The right was claimed of nominating to all the important benefices of England. Foreign ecclesiastics were appointed to rich English livings; and, although they neither resided in the country nor performed any duty therein, they received the revenues from their livings and expended them abroad.

Besides the actual nomination to Church livings when vacant, the Pope, by what was called a reservation, assumed the power of reserving to himself the next presentation to any benefice he pleased; and by another instrument, which he called a provisor, he issued an appointment to such benefice beforehand. The rights of the legal patron were set aside, and he had either to buy up the Pope's provisor or allow his nominee to enjoy the benefice.

In the year 1229, a tenth of the movables of England was demanded, and obtained, to aid the Pope in carrying on a war in which he was engaged. A few years later a fifth was exacted.

In 1352 the parliament requested that "remedy might be had against the Pope's reservations, by which he received the first-fruits from all ecclesiastical dignities, a greater consumption to the country than all the king's wars." In another parliament held in 1376 a protest was made "against the usurpations of the Pope, as being the cause of all the plagues, murrains, famines, and poverty of the land," it being further stated "that the taxes paid to the Pope do amount to five times as much as those paid to the king from the whole realm."

The results of these continual imposts were ruinous to the nation; learning and the arts were discouraged, hospitals fell into decay, the churches became dilapidated, the lands were neglected, and to the latter circumstance Parliament attributed the frequent famines and plagues that visited the people.

Monasteries abounded in the country, and begging friars spread over the land; these still further tending to encourage superstition and to impoverish the people.

The abuses of the papacy did not however go unchallenged. In 1229 the barons refused a pecuniary grant solicited by Gregory IX.; in the reign of Henry III. Grostête, the pious Bishop of Lincoln, raised his voice against the corruption and simony of the Roman See; the evangelical Bradwardine, early in the next century, studied the Scriptures and prayed for the salvation of the Church; stringent Acts were passed, with the view of vindicating the majesty of the law and guarding the property of the nation and the liberties of the subject against the encroachments of Rome. But it was not until the later years of the reign of Edward III. that a successful stand was made against the power of the papacy; and he who was the honoured instrument in God's hands of bringing this to pass, and of bringing to light the Word of Truth, which had so long been hidden from the people, was—John Wicliffe.

> How precious is the Book Divine,
>   By inspiration given;
> Bright as a lamp its doctrines shine,
>   To guide our souls to heaven.
>
> This lamp, through all the tedious night
>   Of life shall guide our way;
> Till we behold the clearer light
>   Of an eternal day.

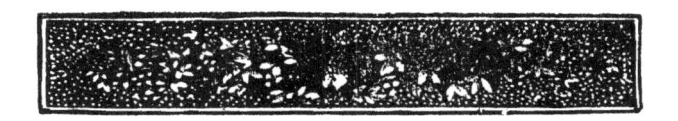

CHAPTER II.

Early Years and College Life.

"The steps of a good man are ordered by the Lord, and he delighteth in His way."—Ps. xxxvii. 23.

THE exact spot where John Wicliffe was born is unknown. It is generally accepted as having been in the hamlet of Spresswell, close to the river Tees, and situated about half-a-mile from the present village of Wicliffe, near Richmond, in Yorkshire. Spresswell itself and its ancient chapel which were both in existence in the eighteenth century, have passed away; but the parish church of Wicliffe still stands. In this the future reformer was probably baptised.

The manor-house of the village stood not far from the church. In this dwelt, from the time of the conquest until the beginning of the seventeenth century, the representatives of the Wicliffe family; who were lords of the manor and patrons of the rectory. From this ancient family John Wicliffe traced his descent, though, perhaps as a protest against his career, his name does not appear in the records of the house, and his relatives seem to have distinguished themselves, after his death, by their staunch adherence to the papacy.

The date of his birth is, according to the usual tradition, the year 1324; but probably it should be fixed a few years earlier. He was named John, and according to the custom of the age, was called after the place of his residence,—John de Wicliffe, or John of Wicliffe.

His home was situated amidst scenery of great and varied beauty, combining the bold and rugged hills and highlands of the North Riding of Yorkshire, with the soft and charming landscapes of the valley of the Tees; and doubtless the strongly marked characteristics of the people amongst whom he dwelt deeply impressed his boyish mind. Probably the sturdy courage and tenacity of purpose which he evinced in after life may be traced to the influences by which he was surrounded, as he dwelt among the old Anglo-Saxon people of those North Yorkshire dales, and drank in the historical recollections and traditions of men who, through all the changes brought about by the Norman invasion, retained their hold upon that portion of the kingdom.

Of Wicliffe's early years and education very little is recorded. While still young he was destined for the Church. From the parish priest, or at one of the schools for elementary instruction—which at that time were freely scattered over the country, in connection with the cathedral towns and the religious orders—he probably received his first lessons, and became acquainted with Latin, also acquiring a slight knowledge of Grammar, Rhetoric, and Logic, and possibly Music, Arithmetic, Geometry, and Astronomy, as they were then taught.

When about sixteen he was sent to Oxford. At that time this city contained five colleges, or "halls," as they were then called: Merton, Balliol, Exeter, Oriel, and University; and about the date of Wicliffe's arrival, nearly 30,000 students were studying there.

Some uncertainty exists as to which of the colleges he first entered, Lechler, the eminent German biographer, maintaining that it was Balliol, while others claim the honour for Merton. Merton was then the most distinguished for its learning of all the colleges in this country, and ranked next to the famous University of Paris. Two of its scholars, William Occam and Duns Scotus, had shed especial lustre upon it; while Bradwardine, who was closing his career about the time that the young Wicliffe was opening his in Oxford, had been one of its professors.

Bradwardine was one of the greatest mathematicians and astronomers of his day; but besides this he was deeply versed in the truths of Scripture, and as a theologian he became more renowned than he had been as a philosopher. He unfolded to his students the way of life, and warned them against substituting a worship of mere external forms and ceremonies in place of the true worship of the heart. The fame of his lectures filled Europe; and his evangelical views, diffused by his scholars, helped to prepare the way for Wicliffe and others who were to come after him.

Meanwhile the young scholar made rapid progress; a quick apprehension, a penetrating intellect, and a retentive memory enabled him to master the various subjects he undertook, and he speedily became proficient in the learning of those days.

Latin he wrote with fluency; but as Greek was seldom taught at that time and little known, he appears to have gained but a slight knowledge of that language. He devoted much time to logic and to the philosophy of the age, and also studied the canon and civil law with great success. Foxe states "that he was famously reputed for a famous divine, a deep schoolman, and no less expert in all kinds of philosophy." Walden, his bitter enemy, writing to Pope Martin II., says, "that he was wonderfully astonished at his most strong arguments, with the places of authority which he had gathered, and with the vehemency and force of his reasons"; and Knighton, the historian, also an enemy, affirms "his powers of debate to have been almost more than human."

It is as a theologian, however, that Wicliffe merits the gratitude of all succeeding ages. At that time it was not necessary to read the Bible as a preparation for the priesthood. The Bachelors of Theology of the lowest grade held readings in the Word of God; but those of the middle and higher ranks considered it beneath their dignity to expound so elementary a book as the Scriptures. They devoted their attention to the Sentences of Peter Lombard, a scholar of the twelfth century who made a collection of the opinions of the fathers, or to disquisitions upon speculations of their own. "There was no mention," says Foxe, "nor almost any word spoken of Scripture. Instead of Peter and Paul, men occupied their time in studying Aquinas and Scotus, and the Master of Sentences."

But Wicliffe loved the Bible, and by-and-by he became known as the "Gospel Doctor."

In the midst of the grovelling superstitions which then abounded, men were startled by the approach of a terrible pestilence. Appearing first in Tartary, it ravaged various kingdoms of Asia, and then passed onwards to Europe. Italy's beautiful cities were turned into charnel-houses. Crossing the Alps, it entered Northern Europe and soon appeared in England.

In August, 1348, it broke out in Dorchester, and on the 1st of November in the same year it reached London. One hundred thousand of the inhabitants of that city perished. The infected generally expired within a few hours; the strongest failed after the second or third day. The lower animals were attacked, and their decaying carcases covered the fields. Husbandry was suspended, the courts of justice were closed, parliament did not meet; everywhere reigned terror, mourning and death.

This terrible visitation made a deep impression upon Wicliffe. He frequently referred to it in after life. It sounded like the trumpet of the Judgment Day in his heart, and he felt how awful a thing it was to die. His burdened soul found relief in the study of the Scriptures, and the struggles which he underwent gave him a confidence in God and a conception of the importance of eternal things, which prepared him to face even death and the stake.

Shortly after this, in 1356, he produced his first publication—a small treatise entitled "The Last Age of the Church." He was then about thirty-two. In this, while he deplored the gross corruption of the ecclesiastical system, and anticipated the terrible chastisements of the Almighty in consequence, he pointed out the refuge of the devout, saying, "So when we were sinful and the children of wrath, God's Son came out of heaven, and, praying his Father for His enemies, He died for us. Then much rather shall we be saved, now we are made righteous through His blood."

Of the private life of John Wicliffe very little is recorded. From 1345 to 1365 appears to have been a period of quiet work at Oxford. In 1361, we find him master of Balliol College; and on the 16th of May in the same year he was nominated by his College to the rectorship of Fillingham, a small parish in the county of Lincoln, about ten miles distant from the city of that name.

This appointment did not, however, necessitate his removal from the University. In all probability he continued for all important purposes to reside in Oxford, and continued a member of the academic body of that city, exercising all the powers and privileges belonging to him as such. An entry exists in the Acts of the See of Lincoln, from which it appears that Wicliffe applied for and obtained, in 1368, the consent of his Bishop to an absence of two years from his parish church of Fillingham in order to devote himself to his studies at Oxford.

Although this portion of the reformer's life has been called his quiet work at Oxford, it was none the less important. As an active member of the governing body of his College, and also of the whole University, he acquired and exercised skill as an administrator; while as a professor he gave disputations and lectures in various philosophical subjects. As a Bachelor of Theology he gave lectures on the Bible; and while others were placing it aside as a book of secondary importance, he held it up as the final standard of appeal, and drew from it truths of the greatest importance to himself and of blessing for his countrymen.

The nomination to the rectorship of Fillingham obliged Wicliffe to relinquish his appointment as Master of Balliol; but in 1365 he was appointed by Simon Islip, the Archbishop of Canterbury, to be warden of Canterbury Hall, a new college founded by that primate a short time previously. The Archbishop, who was an old fellow-student of the reformer, gave as his reasons for appointing him to this office, "his practical qualifications of fidelity, circumspection, and diligence; as well as his learning and estimable life."

A year after this appointment Islip died, and was succeeded as primate by Peter Langham, previously Abbot of Westminster and a private monk. The new archbishop arbitrarily displaced Wicliffe from his office and appointed a new head for Canterbury Hall. This being unjust and in direct opposition to the will of the founder of that college, Wicliffe appealed to the Pope. But Langham had the greater influence at Rome, and after a long delay the Pontiff, in 1370, gave his decision against the reformer.

> Never hasting, never resting,
> Glad in peace and calm in strife ;
> Quietly thyself preparing
> To perform thy part in life.
>
> Earnest, hopeful, and unswerving,
> Weary though thou art and faint,
> Ne'er despair, there's One above thee,
> Listing ever to thy plaint.

CHAPTER III

The Pope or the King.

"Dread not, neither be afraid of them."—DEUT. i. 29

AS yet Wicliffe has appeared before us only as a man of science—a scholar seldom leaving the precincts of Oxford. We are now about to see him step out from the quiet places of the university city and take a leading part in momentous public affairs. The change, although somewhat surprising, does not denote any alteration in him who was the subject of it. Wicliffe had a great mind; he was a man of high mark and possessed a powerful personality. The scholar will now be merged into the patriot, representing in his own person that interpretation of English national feeling which was so conspicuous in the fourteenth century, when crown and people, Norman and Saxon, united, formed a compact body to defend the rights and interests of the kingdom in its external relations, and especially against the Court of Rome.

We have seen how in 1213 King John surrendered the crown of England to Pope Innocent III., and as a sign of his vassalage agreed to pay 1000 marks annually. The oath of fealty was repeated by his son, Henry III., but prudently evaded by succeeding princes; and the tribute was paid, with considerable intermissions, to the close of the minority of Edward III.

Thirty-three years had passed without any payment having been made, and without remonstrance from Rome, when the nation was aroused by the arrival of a letter from Pope Urban V., in 1365, demanding of the English monarch, " the annual payment of a thousand marks, to be transferred to the papal treasury as a feudal acknowledgment for the sovereignty of England and Ireland." In default of such payment the king was admonished " that he would be cited to appear, and to answer for such neglect, in the Court of the Sovereign Pontiff, who had become his civil, no less than his religious superior."

This demand, as unexpected as it was insulting, stirred the nation to its depths. The England of Edward III. was not the England of King John. During the century which had elapsed since Magna Charta was signed, the nation's growth had been marvellously rapid. England had fused Norman and Saxon into one people; she had formed her language, extended her commerce, reformed her laws, and founded seats of learning which had already become renowned; she had fought great battles, and won brilliant victories; her valour was felt, and her power feared, by the Continental States; and when this summons to do homage as a vassal of the Pope was heard, the nation hardly knew whether to meet it with indignation or with derision.

The conqueror of Cressy and Poictiers was ill-fitted to become the vassal of a Pope. The bold and daring spirit of Edward III. could ill brook the insulting summons from Rome. He acted, however, with the greatest prudence; and, summoning his parliament to meet early in the following year, he laid the Pope's letter before it, and bade it take counsel and say what answer should be returned. This parliament assembled in May, 1366.

Having received the Pope's letter, the estates of the realm requested a day to think over the matter; but on the morrow the Lords Spiritual and Temporal, as well as the Commons, met together and unanimously declared against the claims of the Pontiff.

The debate in the parliament was full of importance for England. Wicliffe was present, and, in a tract which was issued shortly afterwards, has preserved a summary of the speeches:—

The first member to rise was a military baron. " The kingdom of England " said he " was won by the sword, and by the sword has it been defended. Let the Pope then gird on his sword and come and try to exact this tribute by force, and I, for one, am ready to resist him."

A second baron rose. " He only," continued he, " is entitled to secular tribute who legitimately exercises secular rule, and is able to give secular protection. The Pope cannot legitimately do either; he is a minister of the Gospel, not a temporal ruler."

"The Pope," said the third speaker, "calls himself the servant of the servants of God. Very well: he can claim recompense only for service done. But where are the services which he renders to this land? Does he minister to us in spirituals? Does he help us in temporals? Does he not rather greedily drain our treasures, and often for the benefit of our enemies? I give my voice against this tribute."

"On what grounds was this tribute originally demanded?" asked another. "Was it not for absolving King John, and releasing the kingdom from interdict? But to bestow spiritual benefits for money is mere simony; it is a piece of ecclesiastical swindling. But if it is as feudal superior of the kingdom that the Pope demands this tribute, why ask a thousand marks? why not ask the throne, the soil, the people of England?"

"Pope Urban tells us," urged another member, "that all kingdoms are Christ's, and that he, as His vicar, holds England for Christ; but as the Pope is liable to sin, and may abuse his trust, it appears to me that it were better that we should hold our land directly and alone of Christ."

The last speaker said: "Let us go at once to the root of this matter. King John had no right to give away the kingdom of England without the consent of the nation. That consent was never given. If John gave his subjects to Innocent like so many chattels, Innocent may come and take his property if he can. We, the people of England, had no voice in the matter; we hold the bargain null and void from the beginning."

Thus spake the parliament of Edward III. In bold and pithy language they declared for the King and rejected the Pope. Their decision ran as follows: " Forasmuch as neither King John, nor any other king, could bring his realm and kingdom into such thraldom and subjection but by common assent of parliament, the which was not given, therefore that which he did was against his oath at his coronation, besides many other causes. If, therefore, the Pope should attempt anything against the king by process, or other matters in deed, the king, with all his subjects, should with all their force and power resist the same."

This decision was unanimous. Not a voice was heard in defence of Urban's arrogant demand. From this time the Pope never explicitly claimed temporal jurisdiction over England.

How far did Wicliffe influence the parliament of Edward III. in arriving at this important conclusion? That he had prepared the way for it by his teaching at Oxford seems certain, but that his influence was more immediately exerted in connection with the present decision appears evident from the fact that very shortly afterwards a doctor of theology, a monk, whose name is unknown, challenged Wicliffe, singling him out by name, to refute certain propositions advanced by this monk in defence of the papal claims.

Why specially single out the reformer, unless he had become a marked man in connection with this controversy?

Whether Wicliffe was actually a member of this parliament it is now difficult to decide, but that such was the fact seems probable. Six masters of arts were returned to represent the inferior clergy, and he may have been one of these; or he may have been summoned by the king as a special commissioner on account of his learning and ability. Lechler thinks that the title assumed by Wicliffe in his reply, "The King's Peculiar Clerk," supports the supposition that the king had specially summoned him to parliament.

In the tract which the reformer was called upon to refute, his antagonist first proposed that the Pope, as vicar of Jesus Christ, was the feudal superior of monarchs and the lord paramount of their kingdoms; he then asserted that the sovereignty of England was legally forfeited to the Pope by the failure of the annual tribute, and furthermore, that the clergy, whether considered as individuals or communities, were fairly exempt, both in person and property, from all subjection to the magistrate. The task imposed upon Wicliffe was one full of danger. Nevertheless, he accepted the challenge, and replied to his adversary.

In opening he stated: "But inasmuch as I am the king's peculiar clerk, I the more willingly undertake the office of defending and counselling that the king exercises his just rule in the realm of England, when he refuses tribute to the Roman Pontiff."

After describing himself as a humble and obedient son of the Church, he proposed to affirm nothing that might be reported to her injury or reasonably offend the ears of devout men, and then he stated his grounds of objection to the temporal power of the Pope. These were the natural rights of men, the laws of the realm of England, and the precepts of Scripture. "Already," he said, "a third and more of England is in the hands of the Pope. There cannot be two temporal sovereigns in one country,—either Edward is king or Urban is king. We accept Edward of England, and reject Urban of Rome." Falling back upon the debate in Parliament, he presented a summary of the speeches then made, and thus placing the estates of the realm in the front, and covering himself with the shield of their authority, he showed to all that the question at issue was the affair of the king and the nation, and not a petty quarrel between an unknown monk and an Oxford doctor.

Shortly after this, in 1372, Wicliffe took his degree of Doctor in Divinity,—a distinction more rare in those days than in ours. The circle of his influence was extended, and he began to be regarded as the centre of a new age. A profound teacher, and an eloquent preacher, he demonstrated to the learned during the week what he intended to preach, and on Sunday he preached to the people what he had previously demonstrated. His disputations gave strength to his sermons, and his sermons shed light upon his disputations. He accused the clergy of having banished the Holy Scriptures, and required the re-establishment of their authority in the Church. Loud acclamations crowned these discussions, and the emissaries of Rome trembled when they heard these shouts of applause.

About this time he published his "Exposition of the Decalogue," an explanation of the law contained in the Ten Commandments.

> All unseen, the Master walketh
>   By the toiling servant's side;
> Comfortable words He talketh,
>   While His hands uphold and guide.
>
> Grief, nor pain, nor any sorrow,
>   Rends thy heart to Him unknown;
> He to-day, and He to-morrow,
>   Grace sufficient gives His own.

CHAPTER IV.

Wicliffe's Battle with the Mendicant Friars.

"Woe be to the shepherds of Israel that do feed themselves! should not the shepherds feed the flocks?"—EZEK. xxxiv. 2.

THE resistance of Edward III. and his parliament to the papacy without had not suppressed the papacy within. Monasteries abounded. In too many instances they were the abodes of corruption.

While precluded by their vow of poverty from holding any property as individuals, the monks were permitted as corporate bodies to possess themselves of all the wealth they could acquire. Lands, houses, hunting-grounds, and forests; with the tithings of tolls, orchards, fisheries, kine, wool, and cloth, formed the dowry of the monastery. Curious furniture adorned its apartments; dainty apparel clothed its inmates; the choice treasures of the field, the tree, and the river, covered their tables; while soft-paced mules carried them by day, and luxurious couches bore them at night.

Their head, the abbot, equalled princes in wealth and surpassed them in pride.

Gross irregularities frequently prevailed, and as early as the end of the twelfth century so many disorders existed that the whole credit of the papal hierarchy was shaken.

Besides the regular clergy and monks, the country was over-run by mendicants, or begging friars; orders instituted early in the thirteenth century. The Franciscans and Dominicans, as these orders were called, after their founders, St. Francis and St. Dominic, professed absolute poverty. They lived by begging.

Clad in gowns of coarse woollen cloth, girded with cord or sash, and provided with capacious pockets, they traversed the land, preaching ridiculous fables, stories from the siege of Troy, &c., to all who were willing to listen, and soliciting alms from the faithful. They were emphatically the soldiers of the Pope, marching through Christendom in two bands, but forming one united army.

The Dominicans were divided into two companies; the one went forward to convert heretics, the other, by the terrible power of the inquisition, to slay them. More rapidly than the older orders did these become corrupt, and only about forty years after their institution, Matthew Paris, a contemporary writer, exclaimed, "It is an awful presage that in 300 years, nay in 400 years and more, the old monastic orders have not so entirely degenerated as these fraternities."

The Dominicans first entered England in 1321. They speedily multiplied and spread over the kingdom. Forty-three houses belonging to their order were established, and from their black cloak and hood they became popularly known as the "Black Friars."

The Franciscans by pious frauds endeavoured to monopolise the wealth of the country. "Every year," they said, "St. Francis descends from heaven to purgatory and delivers the souls of all those who were buried in the dress of his order." Numbers assumed his garb in consequence.

These friars used to kidnap children and shut them up in monasteries. Their practices at the universities were so bad that Fitzralph—Chancellor of Oxford in 1333, and Archbishop of Armagh in 1347—affirmed before the Pope "that parents seeing their children to be stolen from them in the universities by these friars do refuse therefore to send them to their studies." He also stated that "whereas in my time there were in the University of Oxford 30,000 students, now there are not to be found 6000." Fitzralph made a special journey to Avignon, where the Pope then resided, and urged his complaints against the mendicants in person; but although they were but too well founded, the Pope took no notice of them, finding the friars indispensable to him, and knowing that they were his most useful agents.

Fitzralph returned to England, and died three years afterwards, in 1360.

Some obscurity exists as to the date when Wicliffe

commenced his attack upon the mendicant friars. The general opinion may be expressed in the words of an anonymous writer, whose manuscript is still extant. He says: "John Wicliffe, the singular ornament of his time, began at Oxford in the year of our Lord 1360, in his public lectures, to correct the abuses of the clergy and their open wickedness, King Edward III. being living, and continued secure a most valiant champion of the truth against the tyrants of Sodom."

Subsequent investigations, however, lead to the conclusion that the conflict was not entered upon until a later date, probably as late as the year 1378, and it continued until the reformer's death. The evils with which Wicliffe charged the mendicants were summarised and published in his tract entitled "Objections to Friars." This was issued about 1382. In it Wicliffe accused them of "holding fifty heresies and errors, and many more if men would seek them well out."

Among the fifty heresies and errors laid to their charge were the following:—

"Friars say that their religion is more perfect than the religion of Christ, and that it is more meritorious to give alms to hypocrites, that say they are holy and needy when they are strong in body and have overmuch riches, than to give them to poor feeble, crooked, blind, and bed-ridden men."

"Friars draw children to their private order by hypocrisy, lying, and stealing."

"Friars, that be called Masters of Divinity, live as

lords and kings, and send out idiots, full of covetousness, to preach, not the Gospel, but chronicles, fables, and lies; to please the people, and to rob them."

"Friars deal not faithfully in showing people their sins, but flatter them and nourish them in sin."

In reference to this Fitzralph declared : " I have in my diocese of Armagh about 2000 persons who stand condemned by the censures of the Church denounced every year against murderers, thieves, and such-like malefactors, of all which number scarce fourteen have applied to me, or to my clergy, for absolution ; yet they all receive the sacraments, as others do, because they are absolved, or pretend to be absolved, by friars."

Wicliffe continued :—

"Friars praise more their rotten habit than the body of the Lord Jesus Christ ; for they teach lords and ladies that if they die in the habit of St. Francis they shall never go to hell."

He also accused them of making the land lawless, of being Iscariot's children, betraying the truth of the Gospel for money, of maintaining that Holy Scripture is false, of exalting themselves above Christ, of being guilty of simony, and of cruelly persecuting, even unto death, those who, not of their order, travelled the country sowing God's Word among the people.

Besides these charges, he held them up to reprobation, declaring :—

"Friars are most perilous enemies of the Church and of the land ; they hinder curates of their offices and spend needlessly 60,000 marks a-year which they rob the poor people of." And again: "Friars build many churches, and costly waste-houses, and cloisters, as it were castles, and that without need, whereby parish churches and common ways have been impaired and in some cases undone."

While laying bare the vices of the mendicants, Wicliffe also preached the Gospel to his countrymen. The friars claimed, in the name of the Pope, to grant men pardon for their sins. The fallacy of this claim he exposed, but, at the same time, he pointed them to Him who alone could grant pardon for sin. "There cometh," said he, "no pardon but of God. There is no greater heresy than for a man to believe that he is absolved from his sins if he give money, or if a priest lay his hand upon his head and say that he absolveth thee; for thou must be sorrowful in thy heart and make amends to God, else God absolveth thee not."

"May God of His infinite mercy," said he, "destroy the pride, covetousness, hypocrisy, and heresy of this feigned pardoning, and make men busy to keep His commandments, and to set fully their trust in Jesus Christ."

In thus opposing the begging friars, the reformer ran great hazard. Their power was immense. For nearly two centuries the inquisition had been performing its work of torture and destruction on the Continent. During that period its odious business had devolved chiefly upon the orders of St. Dominic and St. Francis, and these, while appealing to the rack and to the stake as their ultimate weapons of debate, are described as "the confessors, the preachers, and the rulers commonly of all men."

But while the danger was great, the good that resulted from this controversy was also great. The mendicants pleaded the sanction of the Saviour for their begging. "Christ and His apostles," said they, "were mendicants and lived on alms." Men turned to the New Testament to see if it were so, and thus became more deeply acquainted with the Word of God. Wicliffe, especially, was led to a yet closer study of the Bible. The truths of Scripture were revealed to him more and more plainly, and he was led to see how widely the Church of Rome had departed from the Gospel of Christ. The preparation for his great work was nearly complete, and, ere long, the Professor of Oxford will give place to the Reformer of England.

> Shall I, for fear of feeble man,
> The Spirit's course in me restrain ?
> Or, undismayed in deed and word,
> Be a true witness for my Lord ?
>
> My life, my blood, I here present,
> If for Thy truth they may be spent :
> Fulfil Thy sovereign counsel, Lord !
> Thy will be done, Thy name adored !
>
> Give me Thy strength, O God of Power !
> Then let winds blow, or thunders roar,
> Thy faithful witness will I be ;
> 'Tis fixed ; I can do all through Thee.

CHAPTER V.

Wicliffe appointed a Royal Commissioner.

"Them that honour me I will honour."—1 SAM ii. 30.

IN this age of liberty it is difficult to imagine the arbitrary power exercised by the Popes of the Middle Ages. In England during the fourteenth century a battle was constantly being carried on between the King and his Parliament on the one side, and the Papal Court on the other.

We have seen how the Parliament in 1366 rejected the demand for the 1000 marks annually, made by Urban V. We have noticed how the country was being drained by the constant exactions of the Roman Pontiffs, and have stated that stringent laws were passed to protect the rights of the Crown and the property of the subject. We have now to witness a continuance of the strife, and to see the measures adopted by tne estates of the realm to throw off the yoke which papal tyranny had imposed upon the nation.

Two Acts had been passed; the first, called the Statute of Provisors, in 1350, and the second, the Statute of Præmunire, three years after, especially with the view of checking the papal usurpations.

The first of these statutes declared it illegal to procure any presentation to any benefice from the Court of Rome, or to accept any living otherwise than as the law directed through the chapters and ordinary electors. The second forbade all appeals on questions of property from the English tribunals to the courts at Rome, under pain of confiscation of goods and imprisonment during the King's pleasure.

In spite of these enactments the Pope continued to reserve to himself certain benefices in England, generally the more wealthy livings, and not only appointed to the same, but by his provisor issued his appointment beforehand. The rights of the Crown, or of the lawful patron, were set aside, and the real presentee had either to buy up the provisor or allow the Pope's nominee, often a foreigner, to enjoy the benefice.

In this way the best livings in England were held by Italians, Frenchmen and other foreigners; some of them being mere boys, ignorant not only of the English language but even of Latin; who never so much as saw their churches, but committed the care of them to such as they could get to serve them the cheapest, and received the revenues at Rome or elsewhere, remitted to them by their proctors to whom they let their tithes.

These grievances were felt to be intolerable. The

Parliament addressed a new remonstrance to the King, setting forth the unbearable nature of the oppressions, and praying him to take action in the matter. Edward III., in 1373, appointed four commissioners to proceed to Avignon, where Pope Gregory XI. resided, to lay the complaints of the English people before him, and to request that for the future he would forbear meddling with the reservation of benefices. The ambassadors were courteously received, but they obtained no redress.

The Parliament renewed their complaints, and requested that "remedy be provided against the provisions of the Pope, whereby he reaps the first fruits of ecclesiastical dignities, the treasure of the realm being thereby conveyed away, which they cannot bear."

In 1374 a Royal Commission was issued to inquire into the number of ecclesiastical benefices and dignities, in England, held by aliens, and to estimate their value. It was found that the number of livings in the hands of Italians, Frenchmen, and other foreigners was so great that, says Foxe, "were it all set down, it would fill almost half-a-quire of paper."

The king resolved to make another attempt to settle this matter with the Papal Court. He appointed a new commission, and it is an evidence of the growing influence of Wicliffe that his name stands second on the list of delegates. The commissioners were John Gilbert, Bishop of Bangor; John Wicliffe, Doctor of Theology; John Guter,

Dean of Segovia; Simon Multon; William Burton; Robert Belknap; and John of Kensyngton.

The Pope declined to receive the King's Commissioners at Avignon, and made choice of the city of Bruges in the Netherlands; and thither he sent his nuncios to confer with the English delegates. The negotiations dragged on for two years, the result being a compromise; the Pope engaging on his part to desist from the reservation of benefices, and the King promising on his, no more to confer them by simple royal command.

This arrangement left the power of the Pope over English benefices at least equal to that of the sovereign. The result satisfied no one in England. The truce was seen to be a hollow one, and did not last.

There is reason to suspect that the interests of England were betrayed in this negotiation. The Bishop of Bangor, on whom the embassy chiefly devolved, was immediately on his return home translated to the see of Hereford, and in 1389 to that of St. David's. In both instances his promotion was the result of papal provisors, and looked like a reward for services rendered.

The visit to Bruges was an important one for the reformer. Wicliffe had never before left his native land. The city to which he went was a large and wealthy one, with a population of 200,000. It was the emporium of Europe. Its citizens combined a taste for splendour with a spirit of independence, and evinced a self-confidence and fearlessness which passed with the more patient victims of feudal tyranny for presumption and insolence. At the time of Wicliffe's visit the conference for the settlement of peace between England and France was sitting in Bruges. The Dukes of Anjou and Burgundy, brothers of the sovereign, were delegates on the part of France: while the claims of England were entrusted to the Earl of Salisbury; Sudbury, then Bishop of London; and John of Gaunt, the Duke of Lancaster, son of the King. Wicliffe's position at Bruges secured him access to these ambassadors, and to other persons of note who were then in the city; and his insight into the policy and intrigues of the States and the Church produced no doubt deep impressions upon his mind, not altogether favourable to the papacy and its friends.

He was more than disgusted with the result of the protracted negotiations, and the views which had been opened to him of papal sanctity were such that his rebukes of the corruptions of the Pope and the Papal Court were soon after his return applied with unsparing severity. Avarice, ambition, hypocrisy— these were the gods that were worshipped at the Roman Court; these were the virtues that adorned the Papal Throne.

Soon after his return from Bruges, Wicliffe was appointed to the rectorship of Lutterworth, in Leicestershire. As this preferment came from the King, it may be accepted as a sign of the royal approval of his conduct as a commissioner, and of his growing influence at Court.

Parliament in April, 1376, re-stated the grievances of the country in relation to the papal demands and encroachments. They drew up a Bill of Indictment against the papal usurpations, and set forth the manifold miseries under which the country was groaning through the tyranny of a foreign power which had crept into the kingdom under spiritual pretexts. In this document it was stated that the revenue drawn by the Pope from the realm was five times as much as that which the King received; that the Pope's collector had opened an establishment in London, with a staff of officers, as if it were one of the great courts of the nation, transporting to the Pope twenty thousand marks annually, or more; and that the Pope often imposed a special tax upon the clergy, which he sometimes expended in subsidising the enemies of the country.

They further stated that it would be good to renew all the statutes against provisions from Rome, and requested that no papal collector or proctor should remain in England, upon pain of life and limb; and that no Englishman, on the like pain, should become such collector or proctor, or remain at the Court of Rome.

The nation supported the Parliament, and the statutes against the papal appointments were rigidly enforced. The Pope maintained the strife for a few years, but ultimately had to give way before the firm attitude of the people.

Wicliffe's was the spirit that moved the Commons of England. His graphic style may be recognised in the document of the Parliament; and he it was who once again led the way to victory and to the assertion of the people's rights as the free subjects of an independent realm.

Prior to these events, the Parliament had in 1371 carried a motion imposing a war-tax upon the estates of the clergy, and, in connection with the imposition of this tax, they had made a proposition to the Crown that the King should remove all prelates from the high offices of State, and fill up the vacancies with laymen. Edward III. accepted the proposal, and in February 1372 none but laymen constituted the Privy Council. Among those who resigned their offices in connection with this proposition were William of Wykeham, the famous architect, who was the Lord Chancellor, and the Bishop of Exeter, who was then the Treasurer of the Kingdom.

In the creation of the feeling which brought about this great and beneficial change, Wicliffe was one of the most important factors. His language is definite: "Neither prelates nor doctors, priests nor deacons, should hold secular offices, that is, those of Chancery, Treasury, Privy Seal, and other such secular offices in the Exchequer. Neither be stewards of lands, nor stewards of the hall, nor clerks of the kitchen, nor clerks of accounts; neither be occupied in any secular office in lords' courts, more especially while secular men are sufficient to do such offices."

In another treatise he writes that "prelates and great religious possessioners are so occupied in heart about worldly lordships and with pleas of business, that no habit of devotion, of praying, of thoughtfulness on heavenly things, on the sins of their own hearts, or on those of other men, may be preserved, neither may they be found studying and preaching of the Gospel, nor visiting and comforting of poor men."

>He liveth long who liveth well!
>　All other life is short and vain;
>He liveth longest who can tell
>　Of living most for heavenly gain.
>
>He liveth long who liveth well!
>　All else is being flung away;
>He liveth longest who can tell
>　Of true things truly done each day.

CHAPTER VI.

Persecution.

"Blessed are they which are persecuted for righteousness' sake : for their's is the kingdom of heaven."—MATT. v. 10.

THE eminent services which Wicliffe rendered to his country, and the bold stand that he maintained against the temporal power of the Pope, caused him to be held in the highest esteem by the nation, but brought upon him the vengeance of the Pontiff and the papal party.

On the 3rd of February, 1377, at the instance of Courtenay, Bishop of London, he was cited to appear on the 19th of the same month, in Our Lady's Chapel in St. Paul's, to answer for his teaching.

As the day drew near, rumour spread abroad of what was about to take place, and when the time arrived a large crowd had assembled at the door of the cathedral.

Attended by two powerful friends,—John of Gaunt, the Duke of Lancaster; and Lord Percy, the Earl Marshall of England,—Wicliffe appeared at the outside of the assemblage. The Duke of Lancaster and Wicliffe had met at Bruges, and the Duke held the reformer in high esteem, on political if not on religious grounds. He therefore accompanied him, and resolved to show him countenance before the tribunal of the bishops.

The three friends found it a difficult matter to make way through the crowd, which not only lined the approaches to the church, but filled its aisles. In forcing a passage, something like an uproar took place. At last, Wicliffe and his supporters entered the Chapel of Our Lady, where the clerical judges were assembled in their robes and insignia of office.

Lechler thus describes the appearance of the reformer:—" Here stood Wicliffe in the presence of his judges, a meagre form dressed in a long light mantle of black cloth, similar to those worn at this day by doctors, masters, and students in Cambridge and Oxford, with a girdle round the middle; his face, adorned with a long thick beard, showed sharp, bold features, a clear piercing eye, firmly-closed lips, which bespoke decision; his whole appearance full of great earnestness, significance, and character."

The haughty Courtenay watched the movements of Wicliffe and his friends, and beheld with displeasure the humble Rector of Lutterworth accompanied by the two most powerful men in England. Turning to the Earl Marshall he said:—

"Percy, if I had known what masteries you would have kept in this church, I would have stopped you from coming in hither."

"He shall keep such masteries," gruffly said John of Gaunt, "though you say nay."

"Sit down, Wicliffe," said Percy, having but scant reverence for a court which owed its authority to a foreign power—"sit down; you have many things to answer to, and have need to repose yourself on a soft seat."

"He must and shall stand," said Courtenay, still more irritated; "it is unreasonable that one on his trial before his ordinary should sit."

"Lord Percy's proposal is but reasonable," exclaimed the Duke of Lancaster; "and as for you," said he, turning to Bishop Courtenay, "who are grown so arrogant and proud, I will bring down the pride not of you alone, but that of all the prelacy in England."

"Do me all the harm you can," was the Bishop's haughty reply.

"You are insolent, my lord," rejoined the Duke, "You think, no doubt, you can trust on your family, but your relations will have trouble enough to protect themselves."

To this the Bishop replied: "My confidence is not in my parents, nor in any man, but only in God, in whom I trust, and by whose assistance I will be bold to speak the truth."

We quote D'Aubigné for what further took place: "Lancaster, who saw hypocrisy only in these words, turned to one of his attendants and whispered in his ear, but so loud as to be heard by the bystanders, 'I would rather pluck the Bishop by the hair of his head out of his chair, than take this at his hands.'

"Lancaster had hardly uttered these imprudent words before the Bishop's partisans fell upon him and Percy, and even upon Wicliffe, who alone had remained calm. The two noblemen resisted, their friends and servants defended them, the uproar became extreme, and there was no hope of restoring tranquillity. The two lords escaped with difficulty, and the assembly broke up in great confusion.

"On the following day, the Earl Marshal having called upon Parliament to apprehend the disturbers of the public peace, the clerical party uniting with the enemies of Lancaster, filled the streets with their clamour; and while the Duke and the Earl escaped by the Thames, the mob collected before Percy's house, broke down the doors, searched every chamber, and thrust their swords into every dark corner. When they found that he had escaped, the rioters, imagining that he was concealed in Lancaster's palace, rushed to the Savoy, at that time the most magnificent building in the kingdom. They killed a priest who endeavoured to stay them, tore down the ducal arms, and hung them on the gallows like those of a traitor. They would have gone still further if the Bishop had not very opportunely reminded them that they were in Lent.

"As for Wicliffe, he was dismissed with an injunction against preaching his doctrines. But this decision of the priests was not ratified by the people of England. Public opinion declared in favour of the reformer. 'If he is guilty,' said they, ' why is he not punished? If he is innocent, why is he ordered to be silent. If he is the weakest in power he is the strongest in truth!'"

The issues of this affair were favourable to the Reformation. The cause of Wicliffe began to be more widely discussed and better understood by the nation. The designs of his enemies had been thwarted, but their hostility increased. They sent nineteen articles selected from his writings, from his divinity lectures, and from his private conversations, to Rome, to Pope Gregory XI. These articles consisted of statements opposed to the doctrine of the Pope's temporal power, and to the worldly possessions of the hierarchy. They also denied the power of the Pope or the Bishop to excommunicate any man, unless by sin he had first made himself obnoxious to God. They likewise declared that every priest truly ordained was competent to administer every sacrament, and asserted that the highest dignitaries, not excepting the Pontiff himself, might be lawfully corrected by their inferiors and even by laymen.

Speedy condemnation followed the receipt of these articles, and five separate bulls were drafted on the same day, 22nd May, 1377, and despatched to England. Three of these were addressed to the Archbishop of Canterbury and to the Bishop of London, the fourth solicited the aid of the King, and the fifth demanded the prompt obedience of the University of Oxford.

Events happened, however, which caused the publication of these bulls to be delayed. On the 21st June, 1377, Edward III. died and was succeeded by his grandson Richard II., a child eleven years of age. His mother, the dowager Princess of Wales, was a woman of spirit, friendly to the sentiments of Wicliffe.

The first Parliament of the new king assembled in October, two months after his accession to the throne. It was animated by a strong spirit of antagonism to Rome. Wicliffe was summoned to its councils. His influence was growing. The trusted commissioner of princes, the counsellor of Parliaments, he was a power in England. A more opportune moment must be waited for before the bulls against him are made public.

The encroachments of the Pontiffs, and the lightening of the burdens imposed upon the nation through the long-continued war with France, formed the chief subjects of attention in the new Parliament. The complaints against the papal provisions and reservations were renewed, and it was proposed that all foreigners, whether monks or seculars, should leave the kingdom, and their lands and property be applied to war purposes.

The question of the right of the country to retain its treasures, in case of necessity, though the same should be demanded by the Pope under pain of his censures, was also discussed.

The Popes at this time dwelt at Avignon, and were Frenchmen. Their sympathies were with their countrymen in the war then waging between France and England, and part of the wealth drained from the latter country went to help its adversary to carry on the war. Not only was the nation drained of its wealth, but that wealth was turned against the country from which it was taken. This was felt to be unendurable.

The following question was submitted to the judgment of Wicliffe by the Parliament :—" Whether the kingdom of England might not lawfully, in case of necessity, detain and keep back the treasure of the kingdom for its defence, that it be not carried away to foreign and strange nations, the Pope himself demanding and requiring the same, under pain of censure ? "

This question appears, in the light of the nineteenth century, a very simple one; but in the fourteenth century the best and bravest of our forefathers were scared by the threat with which the Pope accompanied his demand; and they dared not refuse it until assured by Wicliffe that it was a matter in which the Pope had no right to command, and one in which they incurred no sin, and no danger, by disobedience.

Wicliffe answered the question in the affirmative. He argued the point on the law of nature and on that of the Bible. God, he said, had given to every society the power of self-preservation; and any power given by God to any society or nation may be used for the end for which it was given. He thence concluded " that our kingdom may justly detain its treasure for the defence of itself, in every case where necessity shall appear to require it." He also led his countrymen to the same conclusion, by showing that every contribution to the papacy was strictly an alms, and that alms were only properly bestowed

Persecution. 63

upon the really necessitous. The Papal Court was rich while England was poor, therefore the wealth of the country might lawfully be retained.

Furthermore, he challenged the Pope, as the Vicar of St. Peter, to prove his right to temporal supremacy. "It may indeed be claimed by you," said he, "in virtue of some other plea, but assuredly by no right or title derived from the apostles. For how could an apostle give unto you that which he did not himself possess?"

In this manner the reformer led his countrymen step by step to deny the temporal power of the Pope, and in doing so to question his right to spiritual authority. Guided by his counsel, the Parliament marched onwards, adopting one bold measure after another. His penetrating genius, his sterling uprightness, his cool, cautious, yet fearless courage, made the humble Rector of Lutterworth a most formidable antagonist, and one whom the Romish hierarchy saw must not be overlooked.

Meanwhile the papal bulls had reached England. That addressed to the King found Edward III. in his grave. That sent to the University received but a cold welcome, Oxford having too great a regard for its own fame to extinguish the brightest luminary it contained. The bull sent to the bishops was, however, hailed with delight, for the adherents of Rome could not but foresee that Wicliffe's teaching, and the acts to which it led, tended to the overthrow of the whole fabric of the Roman power in England.

In these bulls the Pope declared that "information

had been received from persons truly worthy of credit, from which it appeared that John Wicliffe, Rector of Lutterworth, in the diocese of Lincoln, and professor of divinity, with a fearlessness the offspring of a detestable insanity, had ventured to dogmatise and preach in favour of opinions wholly subversive of the Church. For this cause the parties addressed are required to seize the person of the offender, in the name of the Pope; to commit him to prison; to obtain complete information as to his tenets; and transmitting such information to Rome by a trusty messenger, they are to retain the arch-heretic as their prisoner until further instructions should be received concerning him."

Sudbury, who had been advanced to the primacy, summoned Wicliffe to appear before him in April, 1378, to answer for his teaching. The court was to sit in the Archbishop's chapel at Lambeth. The papal commissioners were the Primate and the Bishop of London.

On the day appointed, Wicliffe, unaccompanied by either the Duke of Lancaster or Percy, proceeded to the archiepiscopal palace, situated on the right bank of the Thames, opposite Westminster. A crowd, quite as large, and more friendly to the reformer, than that which besieged the doors of St. Paul's on the occasion of his first appearance, surrounded the palace, and many forced their way into the chapel, proclaiming their attachment to the person and opinions of the Rector of Lutterworth. "Men expected he should be devoured, being brought into the lions' den," remarks Fuller in his "Church History." "The Pope's briefs," said the citizens, "ought to have no effect in the realm without the King's consent. Every man is master in his own house."

While the Primate and his peers were consulting how they might eject or silence the intruders, a messenger entered. It was Sir Lewis Clifford, who had been sent by the queen-mother to forbid the bishops passing sentence upon the reformer.

The threatening aspect of the multitude had produced a feeling of consternation among the bishops; the message brought from the queen-mother caused their dismay to be complete. The proceedings were instantly stopped. "At the wind of a reed shaken," says Walsingham, the historian, describing the scene, "their speech became as soft as oil, to the public loss of their own dignity and the damage of the whole Church. They were struck with such fear that you would think them to be as a man who hears not, or one in whose mouth are no reproofs."

Wicliffe stood the only calm and self-possessed man in all the assembly. A formidable list of charges had been handed to him along with his citation. He handed in a written defence of the tenets imputed to him, introducing his remarks as follows:—"In the first place, I protest publicly, as I have often done, that I resolve with my whole heart, and by the grace of God, to be a sincere Christian; and, while life shall last, to profess and to defend the law of Christ as far as I have power. If through ignorance, or from any other cause, I shall fail in this determination, I ask forgiveness of God, and, retracting the errors, submit with humility to the correction of the Church. And since the notions of children, and of weak persons, concerning what I have taught, are conveyed by others, who are more than children, beyond the seas, even to the Court of Rome, I am willing to commit my opinions to writing. These also I am ready to defend even unto death. In my conclusions I have followed the sacred Scriptures and the holy doctors, both in their meaning and in their modes of expression: this I am willing to show; but should it be proved that such conclusions are opposed to the faith, I am prepared very willingly to retract them."

He then proceeded to deny that the Popes have any political dominion; that their spiritual power is absolute, so as to be judged of none but God; that the Pope has any supremacy over the temporal possessions of the clergy and the religious houses; that the priest has liberty to enforce temporal demands by spiritual censures; and he maintained that the power of the priest in absolving or condemning is purely ministerial; and that absolution will profit no one, unless along with it there comes the pardon of God; nor will excommunication hurt any one unless by sin he has exposed himself to the anger of the Almighty. Wicliffe laboured hard to show the fallacy of the Pope's binding and loosing powers. It was the belief in his authority to admit to heaven or to consign to the intolerable flames of purgatory that enchained the conscience of the nation. Let this be dispelled, and the emancipation of England will have been achieved.

A second time the reformer returned unhurt and uncondemned from the tribunal of his powerful enemies. A second time he was victorious. The court issued a prohibition against the future teaching of the tenets charged against him ; but, as he had given no formal promise to obey it, he continued to declare and spread his doctrines as heretofore.

The subject of the property of the Church engaged much of Wicliffe's attention. About this time we find him proposing to the King and Parliament that there should be a reform of the whole ecclesiastical estate.

The Church was enormously rich. She had, moreover, proclaimed a dogma against that wealth ever being reduced. What was given to the Church was given to God ; whoever withdrew any part of the property of the Church robbed God, and committed the awful sin of sacrilege. A curse rested over the man who subtracted a single acre from her domains or a penny from her coffers. Such was the doctrine propounded.

The grievance occasioned was aggravated by the fact that the large possessions of the clergy were exempt from taxes and public burdens. The clergy might, of their own good pleasure, with the sanction of the Pope, grant a voluntary subsidy if the necessities of the State were great ; but no taxes might be exacted from them, or contributions laid upon them or their churches.

These riches were the source of innumerable evils. The lands of the Church grew wider, while the area which supported the burdens of the State and furnished the revenues of the Crown grew narrower. The ecclesiastical body became corrupt; pride, luxury, indolence, resulted from this enormous wealth.

To Wicliffe's far-seeing mind the very root of the evil was laid bare. The "goods" of the Church,—her broad acres, her cathedrals and conventual buildings, her tithes and revenues,—were not, he affirmed, in any legal or strict sense the Church's property. She neither bought them, nor won them by service in the field, nor did she receive them as an unconditional gift. The Church was but the administrator of this property, the nation was the real proprietor; and the nation was bound, through its representatives the King and Parliament, to see that the Church devoted this wealth to the objects for which it was given to her, otherwise it might be recalled. The ecclesiastic who became immoral and failed to fulfil the duties of his office, forfeited that office with all its emoluments; and the law which applied to the individual applied also to the whole corporation of the Church.

Such in brief was the teaching of Wicliffe as set forth in his writings.

He not only proposed, but he earnestly pleaded with the King and Parliament that the whole estate of the Church should be reformed in accordance with the principles he had enunciated. Let the Church surrender all her possessions and return to the simplicity of her early days, and let her depend upon the free-will offerings of the people.

This change was to be brought about gradually. He proposed that as benefices fell vacant the new appointments should convey no right to the temporalities, and thus in a short time the whole face of England would be changed.

In making these proposals in the age in which he lived, we see the courageous independence which actuated the reformer, and his fidelity to what he held to be the truth. The Bible, he believed, was with him, and, supported by it, he bravely held and avowed his opinions. His peril was great, for the Pope and all his followers were against him; but his faith was in Him who is invisible, and in whose hands are the issues of life.

The wealth of the Church, however, remained untouched. Wicliffe was in advance of his age; and it remained for succeeding generations to recognise the soundness of his views, and to act upon his plan.

> Sow when the tempest lowers,
>   For calmer days may break;
> And the seed in darkness nourished,
>   A goodly plant may make.
> Watch not the clouds above thee,
>   Let the wild winds round thee sweep;
> God may the seed-time give thee,
>   But another hand may reap.

CHAPTER VII.

The English Bible.

"The entrance of Thy words giveth light; it giveth understanding unto the simple."—Ps. cxix. 130.

ON the 27th of March, 1378, Pope Gregory XI. died. A short time before his death he returned to Rome, and thus was terminated the "Babylonish captivity," as the residence of the Popes at Avignon has been called by the Italians.

His successor was elected amidst the threats and tumult of the Roman populace, who demanded a Roman for their Pope. The cardinals elected the Archbishop of Barri, an Italian, who assumed the name of Urban VI.

By his coarse manners, his injudicious severity, and his intolerable haughtiness, he alienated the minds of many from him. The cardinals especially were estranged, and declaring his election null and void, being made under intimidation, they withdrew to Fondi, a city of Naples, and there elected another Pontiff, who was proclaimed as Clement VII.

Thus was created the famous schism in the papacy which for half-a-century divided and scandalised the papal world.

Urban VI. dwelt in the Vatican at Rome, while Clement VII. installed himself at Avignon. Germany and England, and some of the smaller European States, sided with Urban; and France, Spain, Sicily, Cyprus, and Scotland espoused the cause of Clement.

The effects of this controversy were most disastrous, and are thus stated by Mosheim in his "Ecclesiastical History":—"The distress and calamity of these times were beyond all power of description; for not to insist on the perpetual contentions and wars between the factions of the several Popes, by which multitudes lost their fortunes and lives, all sense of religion was extinguished in most places, and profligacy rose to a most scandalous excess. The clergy, while they vehemently contended which of the reigning Popes was the true successor of Christ, were so excessively corrupt as to be no longer studious to keep up even the appearance of religion or decency; and in consequence of all this, many plain, well-meaning people, who concluded that no one could possibly partake of eternal life unless united with the Vicar of Christ, were overwhelmed with doubt, and were plunged into the deepest distress of mind."

Wicliffe was deeply affected by the events of this papal schism. Soon after its commencement he published his tract entitled "On the Schism of the Popes." In this he adverted to the dispute as having divided the hierarchy against itself, and as presenting a powerful inducement to attempt the destruction of those laws and customs which had served so greatly to corrupt the clergy and to afflict the whole Christian community. "Emperors and kings," he states, "should help in this cause to maintain God's law, to recover the heritage of the Church, and to destroy the foul sins of clerks, saving their persons. Thus should peace be established and simony destroyed."

While the rival Popes were launching their anathemas against each other, Wicliffe, who had retired to his country parish, was sowing by the peaceful waters of the Avon, and in the rural homesteads of Lutterworth, that Divine seed which yields righteousness and peace in this world and eternal life in that which is to come.

Wicliffe was a true pastor. He preached the Gospel to the poor, and ministered by the bedside of the sick and dying, whether freeman or slave. Nearly three hundred of his sermons remain, having escaped the efforts which were persistently put forth to destroy all that issued from his pen. This sufficiently assures us that his labours as a preacher were most abundant.

In his pulpit discourses, as well as in his writings, from this time forward until his death, he frequently alluded to the lust of dominion, the avarice, and the cruelty of the contending Popes, placing these in fearless contrast with the maxims and spirit of Christ and His apostles.

"Simon Magus," he observed, "never laboured more in the work of simony than do these priests. And so God would no longer suffer the fiend to reign in only one such priest; but for the sin which they had done, made division among two, so that men, in Christ's name, may the more easily overcome them both."

Wicliffe's path was onward. He was repelled from the Popes, whom he feared not to speak of as antichrists, but he was drawn closer to the true Head of the Church, the Lord Jesus. The Bible became increasingly precious, and the reformer now issued his work "On the Truth and Meaning of Scripture." In this he maintained the supreme authority of the Word of God, the right of private judgment, and the sufficiency of Christ's law by itself to rule Christ's Church.

The labours which devolved upon him, and the harassing attacks of his foes, were more than his frame could bear. In 1379 he fell dangerously ill at Oxford. Great was the joy in the monasteries; but for that joy to be complete the heretic must recant. Four regents, representing the four orders of friars, accompanied by four aldermen, were deputed to visit their dying enemy. They hastened to his dwelling, and found him stretched upon his bed, calm and serene. "You have death on your lips," said they; "be touched by your faults, and retract in our presence all that you have said to our injury." Wicliffe remained silent, and the monks flattered themselves with an easy victory. But the nearer the reformer approached eternity the greater was his horror of monkery. The consolation he had found in Jesus Christ had given him fresh energy. He begged his servant to raise him on his couch. Then, feeble and pale, and scarcely able to support himself, he turned towards the friars, who were waiting for his recantation, and opening his livid lips, and fixing on them a piercing look, he said with emphasis, " I shall not die, but live, and again declare the evil deeds of the friars." The monks rushed in astonishment and confusion from his chamber.

Wicliffe's prediction was verified, and he lived to complete the most glorious of his works—the translation of the Scriptures into the language of the people.

The Word of God had been banished into a mysterious obscurity. It is true that several attempts had been made to paraphrase or to translate various portions. The venerable Bede translated the Lord's Prayer and the Gospel of St. John into Saxon in the eighth century; the learned men at Alfred's court translated the four evangelists; Elfric, in the reign of Ethelred, translated some books of the Old Testament; an Anglo-Norman priest paraphrased the Gospels and the Acts; Richard Rolle, "the hermit of Hampole," and some pious clerks in the fourteenth century, produced a version of the Psalms, the Gospels, and the Epistles; but these rare volumes were hidden, like theological curiosities, in the libraries of the convents.

In Wicliffe's time, it was a maxim that the reading

of the Bible was injurious to the laity, and accordingly the priests forbade it. Oral tradition alone preserved among the people the histories of the Holy Scriptures, mingled with legends of the saints.

The result of previous labours in furnishing vernacular versions of the Scriptures is thus summed up by Lechler: " A translation of the entire Bible was never during this whole period accomplished in England, and was never even apparently contemplated. The Psalter was the only book which was fully and literally translated into all the three languages, —Anglo-Saxon, Anglo-Norman, and Old English. In addition, several books of Scripture, especially Old Testament books, were translated partially or in select passages—*e.g.*, by Elfric, leaving out of view poetical versions and the Gospel of St. John, translated by Bede, which celebrated work has not come down to us. Last of all—and this fact is of great importance—in none of these translations was it designed to make the Word of God accessible to the mass of the people, and to spread Scriptural knowledge among them. The only object which was had in view was partly to furnish aid to the clergy, and to render a service to the educated class."

Such was the state of Biblical translation when Wicliffe undertook his great work. His idea was to give the whole Bible in the vernacular to the people of England, so that every man in the realm might read in the tongue wherein he was born the wonderful works of God.

The motives which urged him to this enterprise

may be gathered from some of his writings about this time. In his treatise on the "Truth and Meaning of Scripture," he maintained the sufficiency of Christ's law for all purposes of doctrine, discipline, and daily conduct; and he argued "that a Christian man, well understanding it, may gather sufficient knowledge during his pilgrimage upon earth; that all truth is contained in Scripture; that we should admit of no conclusion not approved there; that there is no court beside the Court of Heaven; that though there were a hundred Popes, and all the friars in the world were turned into cardinals, yet should we learn more from the Gospel than we should from all that multitude; and that true sons will in no wise go about to infringe the will and testament of their Heavenly Father."

Later on he wrote: "As the faith of the Church is contained in the Scriptures, the more these are known in an orthodox sense the better."

A few years only of broken health remained for the accomplishment of his great undertaking; his intellectual vigour, however, was unimpaired. He was ignorant of Greek and Hebrew, but he was a good Latin scholar, and above all he loved the Bible; he understood it, and he desired to communicate its treasures to others.

While the papal world was in commotion, in his quiet Rectory of Lutterworth he set himself down to his task. With the Latin Vulgate open before him —that book which all his life he had studied—he translated verse after verse, rendering into the English tongue those sublime truths which had ever been to him strength, guidance, and consolation.

The whole of the New Testament was translated by himself; but the Old Testament appears to have been translated, under his direction, by one of his friends—probably being carried on while the New was in progress, and the translation effected by Dr. Nicholas Hereford, of Oxford. It was, however, partly revised by Wicliffe.

The grand work was finished by 1382. As a version of the Scriptures it was remarkably truthful and spirited. Hereford's portion was very literal, keeping close to the Latin text, but the books which Wicliffe translated were kept thoroughly in accordance with the spirit of his mother tongue, and the requirements of English readers; the translation therefore is so simple as to be thoroughly readable.

We give, by way of extract, John xiv. verses 1 to 4, as contained in this version:—

"Be not youre herte afraied, ne drede it; ye bileuen in God, and bileue ye in me. In the hous of my fadir ben many dwellyngis; if ony thing lesse, Y hadde seid to you, for Y go to make redi to you a place. And if Y go, and make redi to you a place, eftsoones Y come, and Y schal take you to my silf, that where Y am, ye be. And whidur Y go, ye witen, and ye witen the weie."

The translation ended, the next effort of the reformer was to get the book placed if possible within the reach of all. "When the work of translating was ended," says Dr. Wylie, in his "History of Protestantism," "the nearly as difficult work of publishing began. In those days there was no printing-press to multiply copies by the thousand as in our times, and no publishing firm to circulate these thousands over the kingdom. The author himself had to see to all this. The methods of publishing a book in that age were various. The more common way was to place a copy in the hall of some convent or in the library of some college, where all might come and read, and, if the book pleased, order a copy to be made for their own use. . . . Others set up pulpits at cross ways, and places of public resort, and read portions of their work in the hearing of the audiences that gathered round them, and those who liked what they heard bought copies for themselves. But Wicliffe did not need to have recourse to any of these expedients. The interest taken in the man and in his work, enlisted a hundred expert hands, who, though they toiled to multiply copies, could scarcely supply the many who were eager to buy. Some ordered complete copies to be made for them; others were content with portions; the same copy served several families in many instances, and in a very short time Wicliffe's English Bible had obtained a wide circulation, and brought a new life into many an English home."

In the work of diffusing the Scriptures his "poor priests" doubtless assisted.

The importance of preaching deeply impressed the reformer. "The highest service," said he, "that men may attain to on earth is to preach the Word of God." He saw the begging friars strolling over the country, preaching the legends of saints and the history of the Trojan war, captivating the people, and he felt the need of doing for the glory of God what they did to fill their wallets. Turning to the most pious of his disciples, he said, "Go and preach, it is the sublimest work. After your sermon is ended, do you visit the sick, the aged, the poor, the blind, and the lame, and succour them according to your ability."

These "poor priests," as they were called, set off barefoot, a staff in their hands, clothed in a coarse robe, living on alms, and satisfied with the plainest food. They stopped in the fields near some village, in the churchyards, in the market-places of the towns, and sometimes even in the churches. The people thronged around, as with a popular eloquence they urged them to repentance and pointed out the way of salvation by faith in the Lord Jesus Christ.

One who became widely known, and who in an especial manner gained the affections of the people, was named John Ashton. He might frequently have been seen journeying along the highway engaged in his Master's service, or standing under some tree by the roadside preaching to an attentive crowd, or seated at some lowly cottage hearth telling of the love of Jesus.

These evangelists travelled throughout the land, finding favour with the people, but being persecuted by the Church. In 1382 Knighton, a contemporary writer, asserted that "their number very much increased, and that, starting like saplings from the root of a tree, they were multiplied, and filled every place within the compass of the land."

The doctrines of the reformer were thus disseminated over the country, and they became known to all classes of society. Wicliffe afterwards asserted that a third of the priests of England were of his sentiment on the question of the eucharist, and among the common people his disciples were innumerable. "You could not meet two men on the highway," said one of his enemies, "but one of them was a Wicliffite."

As soon as Wicliffe's translation of the Bible began to be scattered abroad, a great outcry was made by the priests and their followers. He had committed a crime unknown to former ages. He was a heretic, a sacrilegious man; he had broken into the temple and stolen the sacred vessels; he had fired the House of God. Knighton, who was canon of Leicester, reflects the spirit of the clergy when he says, adverting to the zeal of Wicliffe in giving the Scriptures to the people: "Christ delivered his Gospel to the clergy and doctors of the Church, that they might administer to the laity and to weaker persons, according to the state of the times and the wants of men. But this Master John Wicliffe translated it out of Latin into English, and thus laid it more open to the laity, and to women who could read, than it had formerly been to the most learned of the clergy, even to those of them who had the best understanding. And in this way the Gospel pearl is cast abroad, and trodden under foot of swine, and that which was before precious to both clergy and laity is rendered, as it were, the common jest of both. The jewel of the Church is turned into the sport of the people, and what was hitherto the principal gift of the clergy and divines is made for ever common to the laity."

Those who love the Word of God look not, however, upon Wicliffe's act as a crime; they rather count his translation of the Scriptures not only as one of the greatest ornaments of the English language of his age, but as being the noblest monument of himself.

> Search the Scriptures for salvation,
>   Christ the Lord has told us so;
> Every tongue and every nation
>   Should the Holy Bible know;
> God's message 'tis, of love and life
> Sent to a world of sin and strife

CHAPTER VIII.

Transubstantiation.

"The words that I speak unto you, they are spirit, and they are life."—JOHN vi. 63.

WICLIFFE'S great work was accomplished, but his labours were not yet over. A brief period must elapse before he shall be called home to receive his reward. He was old and feeble, and needed repose; but the honour of God and the welfare of his country were dear to his heart, and once more he girded himself for the conflict; this time turning to attack the doctrinal system of the Church of Rome.

The doctrine of Transubstantiation, one of the chief supports of the Romish Church, was brought into England by the Norman priests at the time of the Conquest. In this dogma the Church of Rome teaches "that by the sacramental words duly pronounced by the priest, the bread and wine upon the altar are transubstantiated, or substantially converted into the true body and blood of Christ; so that after consecration there is not in that venerable sacrament the material bread and wine which before existed, considered in their own substances or natures, but only the species of the same, under which are contained the true body of Christ, and His blood—not figuratively, but essentially, substantially, and corporally; so that Christ is verily there in His own proper bodily presence."

In the spring of 1381, Wicliffe posted up at Oxford twelve theses, or short propositions, in which he denied the dogma of transubstantiation, and challenged those of a contrary opinion to debate the matter with him. The first of these theses was as follows: "The consecrated host which we see upon the altar is neither Christ nor any part of Christ, but an efficacious sign of him." Wicliffe argued that the bread and wine were as truly bread and wine after as before their consecration.

The publication of these theses caused great commotion at Oxford. At this time the larger portion of the honours of the University was possessed by the religious orders. All shouted heresy, but no one dared to prove it to the author of the objectionable sentences.

A council of twelve—four secular doctors and eight monks—was summoned by William Barton, the Chancellor of the University, and unanimously condemned Wicliffe's opinions as heretical, and threatened heavy penalties against any one who should teach them in the University or listen to the teaching of them there.

Wicliffe was seated in his chair as professor, lecturing upon the eucharist to his pupils in the School of the Augustinians, when an officer entered and read the sentence of condemnation passed upon him by the council.

For a moment he remained silent; he then rose and said, "You ought first to have shown me that I am in error," and then he challenged his opponents to refute his published opinions.

Receiving for reply that he must either submit to silence or imprisonment, he said, "Then I appeal to the King and the Parliament."

The Duke of Lancaster, becoming alarmed, hastened to his old friend, and begged him—even ordered him —to trouble himself no more about this matter. But the reformer was firm; it might cost him his life, but he would abide by the truth.

As some time must elapse before the Parliament again met, Wicliffe withdrew to Lutterworth; and there, while quietly ministering to his flock, he, by his voice in the pulpit, and by his pen, still further diffused those sacred truths which he had drawn from the Word of God. He now published his tract, entitled "The Wicket," an explanation in English of the words, "This is my body"

In the summer of 1381 the people, oppressed by their heavy burdens, and the severity of the tax-collectors, rose in rebellion, and, led by Wat Tyler and a dissolute priest named Ball, marched upon London. Strengthened by the lower orders of the city, they burnt the magnificent palace of the Duke of Lancaster in the Savoy, and seizing Sudbury the

Primate, then Chancellor of the kingdom, they beheaded him in the Tower. Other officers of State were also condemned to death. In a few days the insurrection was quelled, and its leaders, together with hundreds of their followers, executed.

The enemies of the Reformation endeavoured to lay the blame of this insurrection to the teaching of Wicliffe, and to cast opprobrium upon him and his cause in consequence. But the Gospel incites not to deeds of violence, and the sympathy of the insurrectionists with the mendicant friars—the avowed enemies of Wicliffe—is proof that he was not the one who led the people on to rebellion.

Immediately after the insurrection of Wat Tyler and his followers, Courtenay, the Bishop of London, was made Primate in the place of Sudbury. His translation to the primacy was secured by a bull from Pope Urban VI., and this increased his scrupulous submission to the pleasure of the papacy. He was a most zealous opponent of the reformer, and, as soon as the pall—the badge and insignia by which the Pope conveys to bishops the authority to act in his name—arrived, he convoked a synod to try the Rector of Lutterworth.

The court met on the 17th of May, 1382, in the hall of the Dominican Monastery, Blackfriars, London. It consisted of eight prelates, fourteen doctors, six bachelors of divinity, fifteen mendicant friars, and four monks. Truly an impartial assembly to try the Gospel doctor!

The members had just taken their seats, and were

proceeding to business, when an earthquake shook the city. The monastery trembled. The members of the court, much alarmed, turned to its president, and demanded an adjournment. It seemed as if the Divine displeasure rested upon their inquiry.

The Archbishop skilfully applied this incident to his own purpose. "Know you not," said he, "that the noxious vapours which catch fire in the bosom of the earth, and give rise to these phenomena which alarm you, lose all their force when they burst forth? Well, in like manner, by rejecting the wicked from our community, we shall put an end to the convulsions of the Church." The trial proceeded.

An officer of the court read out twenty-four propositions selected from the writings of the reformer. After the "good deliberation" of three days, it was agreed that ten of these were heretical, and the remainder erroneous. The sentence of this court was sent to the Bishop of London,—the metropolis being scarcely less infected by Wicliffe's doctrines than Oxford,—and to all his brethren, the suffragans of the diocese of Canterbury; and also to the Bishop of Lincoln, in whose diocese Lutterworth was situated; and it was accompanied by the commands of Courtenay, as "Primate of all England," that they should look to it that these pestiferous doctrines were not taught in their dioceses.

Another mandate was addressed to the Primate's Commissioner at Oxford, enjoining him to publish throughout the University the decisions of the synod, and commanding that all persons holding or maintaining the errors specified, be holden in the strictest abhorrence under the penalty of the great anathema. The University was, however, a hot-bed of heresy, and was but little inclined to carry out the commands of the Archbishop. Courtenay, therefore, carried his complaint to the young King, Richard II. "If we permit this heretic," said he, "to appeal continually to the passions of the people, our destruction is inevitable; we must silence these Lollards."

Many circumstances at this time made it appear politic for the Crown to approach nearer to the Church. It was easy, therefore, for such a prelate as Courtenay to prevail. The King gave authority "to confine in the prisons of the State any who should maintain the condemned propositions."

A motion was carried through the House of Lords to this effect, but was not passed by the Commons. Although without the consent of the Commons it could not become law, an ordinance, dated 26th May, 1382, was placed on the statute-book substantially embodying its requirements.

A fierce persecution now commenced against the reformer and his followers. Lancaster, who upheld Wicliffe so long as the struggle was a political one, feared to follow him into the region of heresy. Some of his disciples forsook him; enemies closed around; but his trust was not in man, his hope was in God; and, while persecution was being carried on against those who professed his tenets, and threatened to strike him down himself, he prepared to go yet another step forward.

Parliament re-assembled on the 19th of November, 1382. Wicliffe, who felt that he might be struck down at any moment, resolved that his countrymen should not be ignorant of the opinions for which he suffered. He, therefore, made haste to present his appeal to the King and the Parliament.

In this document he pointed out four grievances, and for each he demanded a very sweeping measure of reform. He first declared against the monastic orders, and pleaded for their abolition; secondly, he asserted that secular lords might lawfully and meritoriously, in many cases, take away temporal goods given to the Church; he next affirmed that even tithes and voluntary offerings should be withdrawn from priests who were guilty of great sins; and in the last he pleaded that the doctrine of the eucharist, as taught by Christ and His apostles, might also be taught openly in the churches.

This appeal made a great impression upon the Commons. They presented a petition to the King requiring that the persecuting statute, obtained by the Primate, might be disannulled, and declaring that it was not their intention that either they themselves or their successors should be further bound to the prelates than were their ancestors in former times. The King granted their request, and the statute was repealed.

Both the Parliament and Convocation were at this time assembled at Oxford. Baffled in the Parliament, Courtenay turned to Convocation. Here he could count upon having a more subservient court.

The clergy assembled were informed "that their business was to grant a subsidy to the Crown; and to remedy certain disorders which had too long disgraced the University, and were rapidly extending to the whole community, of whose spiritual safety they were the properly constituted guardians."

In this meeting the Archbishop had concentrated his whole strength. Six bishops, many doctors in divinity, and a host of inferior clergy, were there; the concourse being swelled by the dignitaries and youths of Oxford. Before this assembly Wicliffe was cited to appear.

Forty years had passed since he entered Oxford as a scholar; its halls had witnessed the toils of his youth and the labours of his manhood; but now it appeared to be turning against him.

He came now to be tried, perhaps condemned; and, if his judges were able, to be delivered to the civil power for punishment as a heretic. A solemn silence reigned as the reformer stood alone before his judges, calm and firm.

The indictment turned specially upon Transubstantiation. Did he affirm or deny that cardinal doctrine of the Church? Lancaster had advised him to submit in all doctrinal matters to the judgment of his order. But he was bound by his conscience and the Word of God, and he could not deny. Raising his venerable head, and looking with his clear, piercing eyes straight at Courtenay, he reproached the priests for disseminating error in order to sell their masses, and then, stopping, uttered these

F

simple but energetic words, "The truth shall prevail."

"Having thus spoken," says D'Aubigné, he prepared to leave the court. His enemies dared not say a word; and like his Divine Master at Nazareth, he passed through the midst of them, and no man ventured to stop him."

Leaving Oxford, he retired once more to Lutterworth.

> And is this all? Can reason do no more
> Than bid me shun the deep and dread the shore?
> Sweet moralist! afloat on life's rough sea,
> The Christian has an art unknown to thee:
> He holds no parley with unmanly fears;
> Where Duty bids he confidently steers,
> Faces a thousand dangers at her call,
> And, trusting in his God, surmounts them all.

CHAPTER IX.

Conclusion.

"Henceforth there is laid up for me a crown of righteousness, which the Lord, the righteous Judge, shall give me at that day."—2 TIM. iv. 8.

WICLIFFE reached Lutterworth in safety. His remaining days were passed in peace, undisturbed by his enemies. Their enmity was unabated, but God in a marvellous manner protected His servant. The schism of the Popes, the political troubles of England, the favour with which the Duke of Lancaster still regarded him, all combined to form a rampart around the reformer.

"His very courage, in the hand of God, was his shield; for, while weaker men were apprehended and compelled to recant, Wicliffe, who would burn but not recant, was left at liberty." He himself expected nothing but imprisonment and death.

In his "Trialogus," written about this time, he said: "We have no need to go among the heathen in order to die a martyr's death; we have only to preach persistently the law of Christ in the hearing of Cæsar's prelates, and instantly we shall have a flourishing martyrdom, if we hold out in faith and patience."

In this work, Truth, Falsehood, and Wisdom were personified, and between them they discussed all the principal religious topics of the day. Truth proposed questions, Falsehood raised objections, and Wisdom declared sound doctrine.

As Wicliffe's weakness increased, he was assisted in his pastoral duties by one of his followers, named John Horn; while another, named John Purvey, became his constant attendant, his diligent co-worker, and his confidential friend. Purvey wrote out and collected many of the reformer's discourses, which have in consequence been preserved, and a few years after Wicliffe's death he revised his translation of the Bible.

During the two years which intervened between his appearance at the Oxford Synod and his death, Wicliffe continued zealously at work. Portions of the Scriptures in the English language, tracts on prayer, on the Catechism, on the doctrines of the Church, on preaching, on pastoral work, on the life and conversation which should characterise priests,— all issued from the Rectory at Lutterworth.

It has generally been stated that, one day during this period, while the reformer was quietly toiling with his pen, he received a summons from the Pontiff to appear at Rome; and that while declining on account of his age and infirmities, to obey the command, he wrote a letter to Pope Urban VI. firmly upholding the truth of the doctrines he had taught. This story, however, seems, upon careful examination, to rest on no basis of authority, and Lechler states that "this alleged citation to Rome must be relegated to the category of groundless traditions."

In 1382 a crusade set forth from England to fight for the cause of Urban VI. against the supporters of the rival Pope, Clement VII. Every effort was made to induce as many as possible to join in this crusade, either personally or by donations. Indulgences were granted, available for both the living and the dead, to all who should assist; while those who opposed this sacred enterprise were anathematised.

Wicliffe viewed these proceedings with shame and displeasure. In the summer of 1383 he published a tract "Against the War of the Clergy," in which he severely condemned the crusade and all connected with it.

The end now drew near. Towards the close of 1382 the reformer had been stricken with paralysis, but from this he partially recovered. He was in his church at Lutterworth, in the midst of his beloved flock, on the last Sunday in 1384, engaged in the administration of the Sacrament of the Lord's Supper. As he was in the act of consecrating the bread and wine, he was again stricken with paralysis, and fell to the ground. His friends affectionately carried him from the church to the rectory, and laid him upon his bed. He continued speechless until the 31st of

December, when he was called up higher; his life and the year 1384 ending together.

His enemies saw in the circumstances of his death the terrible judgment of God, but his friends looked upon this as the glorious conclusion of a noble life. "None of its years, scarcely any of its days, were passed unprofitably on the bed of sickness. The moment his great work was finished, that moment the voice spake to him, which said, 'Come up hither!'"

> Then, with no throbs of fiery pain,
> No cold gradation of decay,
> Death broke at once the vital chain
> And freed his soul the nearest way.

Of the character and opinions of John Wicliffe we have space to say but little. He possessed that combination of opposite qualities which marks the great man. With a keenness that enabled him to follow all the intricacies and subtleties of scholastic argument, he united a temper eminently practical. He penetrated with intuitive insight to the root of all the evils that afflicted England, and with rare practical sagacity he devised and set in motion the true remedies for those evils. The evil he saw was ignorance, the remedy with which he sought to cure it was light. He therefore translated the Bible, and organised a body of pious earnest teachers to spread the truths of the Gospel throughout the land.

As a patriot, he strove to deliver his country from the tyranny of the papacy. He pointed out its true character, and by his influence he led the Parliament

Conclusion.

of England to resist the claims of Rome, and to assert the independence of the nation.

As a scholar, he was unquestionably the most extraordinary man of his age. He occupied the chair of theology in the first seminary of the kingdom, a fact proving his proficiency in the science of the schoolmen; additional evidence of which is afforded by his writings, and also by the reluctant testimony of his enemies. "Not only his adherents, but even his opponents looked upon him as having no living equal in learning and scientific ability; to all eyes he shone as a star of the first magnitude."

As a preacher he was earnest, devout, and faithful. His sermons which have been preserved are of two kinds, those written in Latin, preached before the university, and those written in English, preached to his congregation at Lutterworth and to assemblies of the common people elsewhere. These latter are free from the phraseology of the schools, and are full of intellectual strength, but plain in language, and fresh and vitalising in power.

Above all his other knowledge, Wicliffe possessed a profound acquaintance with the Scriptures. He studied the Bible, he venerated it as the Word of God. He held that it contained a perfect revelation of the Divine will; a full, plain, and infallible rule of both what man is to believe, and what he is to do. He fully received its truths into his heart and governed his actions by its teachings. Turning away from all human guides, he prayerfully and diligently searched the Scriptures to know the will of God, and then bowed to that will with the docility of a child.

Bowing himself to the authority of the Divine Word he endeavoured to get all men to submit to it. His great aim was to bring men back to the Bible. He exalted it as the one great authority before which all should bow, the law which infinitely exceeded all other laws, the book above all other books, for "other writings," he declared, " can have worth or authority only so far as their sentiment is derived from the Scriptures."

Of Wicliffe's personal piety there can be no doubt. It is true that scarcely any memorials of his private life remain, but his public history is an enduring monument of his personal Christianity. Tradition describes him as a most exemplary pastor, devoting a portion of each morning to relieving the needy, and consoling the aged, the sick, and the dying. In his manuscript for the order of priesthood, he states, " Good priests, who live well in purity of thought, speech, and deeds, and in good example to the people, who teach the law of God up to their knowledge, and labour fast, night and day to learn it better, and teach it openly and constantly, these are very prophets of God, and the spiritual lights of the world!" This was his ideal, and his writings and public actions prove that his life agreed thereto.

As an author he was most industrious. Soon after his death it was affirmed that his writings were as numerous as those of Augustine. Like his sermons, his works were written some in Latin, and others in

Conclusion.

English. Notwithstanding all the efforts made to destroy them, large numbers are yet in existence. The libraries of the British Museum, of Trinity College, Dublin, the Bodleian Library at Oxford, the library at Lambeth Palace, the Imperial Library at Vienna, and others, are enriched by the writings of the reformer. His most important work was his translation of the Scriptures, but the "Poor Caitiff," a collection of tracts on practical Christianity, written in English for the instruction of the poorer people, and "The Wicket," before alluded to, became very popular, and produced a profound impression.

Of Wicliffe's doctrines we can give but a very brief summary. He denied the temporal power of the Pope, as well as his claim to be the spiritual head of the Church. He upheld the right of private judgment, when prayerfully and carefully exercised, in the interpretation of Scripture; and declared free remission of sins through the atonement of the Lord Jesus Christ. Sanctification by the aid of the Holy Spirit he taught in the following, as well as in other passages: "All our sufficiency is of God, through the mediation of Jesus Christ, thus of sinful and ungrateful men God maketh good men, and all the goodness in this cometh of God. Nor trouble we about the first cause, since God Himself is certainly the first cause."

While preaching a free salvation through a crucified Saviour he insisted on the necessity for self-denial and holiness, "Christ not compelling," said he, "but freely counselling every man to seek a perfect life, saith, 'Let him deny himself, and take up his cross and follow Me.' Let us then deny ourselves in whatever we have made ourselves by sin, and such as we are made by grace let us continue."

The belief in an intermediate state appears in some of the writings of the reformer, but he denounced with severity the representations that were made of suffering souls in purgatory, and the lucrative trade that was carried on by the priests "inventing new pains, horrible and shameful, to make men pay a great ransom."

The doctrine of the invocation of saints he opposed, and he condemned the worship of images. He held that "confession made to those who are true priests, and who understand the will of God, doth much good to sinful men, so long as contrition for past sins comes therewith"; but his parting advice on this subject was, "confess thyself to God, with constancy and contrition, and He may not fail, He will absolve thee."

The falseness of the doctrine of indulgences he freely exposed. "Prelates," said he, "foully deceive Christian men by their pretended indulgences or pardons and rob them wickedly of their money." Transubstantiation as taught by the Church of Rome, we have already seen, he declared to be contrary to the teaching of Scripture.

Wicliffe foretold that from the bosom of monkery would some day proceed the regeneration of the Church. "If the friars whom God condescends to teach shall be converted to the primitive religion of Christ," said he, "we shall see them abandoning

Conclusion. 103

their unbelief and returning freely, with or without the permission of anti-christ, to the religion of the Lord, and building up the Church as did St. Paul." Thus did his piercing glance discover at the distance of nearly a century and a-half, the young monk, Luther, in the Augustine convent at Erfurt, converted by the Epistle to the Romans, and returning to the spirit of St. Paul and the religion of Jesus Christ.

The Lollards, as the followers of Wicliffe were called, probably from their singing in a low or hushed voice, suffered cruel persecution after his death. Some were burnt, others imprisoned, till at last it seemed as though the leaven of the reformer had been eradicated from England, and that the morning star of the Reformation had shone in vain; but as the wind wafts the seed from one place to another, so the doctrines of John Wicliffe were wafted from Britain to the continent of Europe, and being carried into Bohemia by Jerome of Prague, they were embraced by John Huss, and afterwards took deep root and prepared the minds of the people for the great Reformation of the sixteenth century.

Thirty years had passed since the reformer's death, when the Council of Constance condemned a number of propositions which were said to have been extracted from his writings; and, as it appeared that he died an obstinate heretic, his memory was pronounced infamous, and it was decreed " that his body and bones should be taken from the ground and thrown away from the burial of any church, according to the canon laws and decrees!"

In pursuance of this decree, a few years afterwards his grave at Lutterworth was opened, and his remains removed. These were then burnt, and the ashes cast into the adjoining brook named the "Swift," and Fuller, describing the scene, quaintly but truly says: "This brook conveyed them into Avon, the Avon into the Severn, the Severn into the narrow seas, they into the main ocean; and thus the ashes of Wicliffe were the emblem of his doctrine, which is now dispersed all the world over."

> As thou these ashes, little brook! will bear
> Into the Avon, Avon to the tide
> Of Severn, Severn to the narrow seas,
> Into main ocean they, this deed accursed,
> An emblem yields to friends and enemies,
> How the bold Teacher's doctrine, sanctified
> By truth, shall spread, throughout the world dispersed.

MARTIN LUTHER

THE

REFORMER

MARTIN LUTHER

THE

REFORMER

"Here I stand, I can do no other; may God help me! Amen!

Go forward, Christian soldier:
Fear not the secret foe,
Far more o'er thee are watching
Than human eyes can know;
Trust only Christ thy captain,
Cease not to watch and pray,
Heed not the treacherous voices
That lure thy soul away.

KILMARNOCK, SCOTLAND
JOHN RITCHIE LTD.
PUBLISHERS OF CHRISTIAN LITERATURE
AND THROUGH ALL BOOKSELLERS

CONTENTS.

CHAP.		PAGE
I.	EARLY DAYS,	113
II.	THE STUDENT AT ERFURT,	120
III.	THE MONK,	126
IV.	LUTHER AT WITTEMBERG,	131
V.	THE VISIT TO ROME,	135
VI.	THE INDULGENCES,	140
VII.	THE THESES,	145
VIII.	AUGSBURG,	154
IX.	A TRUCE,	161
X.	THE PAPAL BULL,	166
XI.	THE DIET OF WORMS,	174
XII.	THE WARTBURG,	188
XIII.	RETURN TO WITTEMBERG,	194
XIV.	CLOSING SCENES,	203

MARTIN LUTHER.

CHAPTER I.

Early Days.

"My Father, Thou art the guide of my youth."—JER. iii. 4.

MARTIN LUTHER was born on the 10th November, 1483, in the little town of Eisleben, in Saxony. His parents were very poor; but they feared God, and lived uprightly. John Luther, his father, was a woodcutter; and often his mother, Margaret, carried wood upon her back, so that she might help to get the means for bringing up her children.

When the little boy was about six months old, his parents left Eisleben, and went to live at Mansfeld. Here for some time John Luther worked as a miner, and by steady perseverance managed to save sufficient money to purchase two small furnaces for smelting iron. He was a man fond of books, and sought the society of learned men. Soon afterwards, he was made one of the councillors of Mansfeld, and was able to invite to his table the learned men of the place. The clergy and the schoolmasters were frequent guests; and while these dined with his father, young Martin was allowed to remain in the room. This greatly pleased him, and it was his ambition one day to become a schoolmaster or a learned man.

As soon as their son was old enough to be taught, his parents sought to teach him to know God, and to train their child up in His fear. Often would his father kneel by his bedside and pray aloud, asking the Lord that his boy might remember His name, and one day contribute to the propagation of the truth.

By-and-by we shall see how the good father's prayers were answered.

While still very young, the lad was sent to school, and often might little Martin have been seen carried in his father's arms, or in the arms of a friend, on his way to the schoolmaster's house. We do not know whether he liked school; perhaps he did not, for the discipline was very severe. He was clever, but impetuous and sometimes obstinate; and often, both at home and at school, was severely chastised. His mother on one occasion beat him till the blood came, and his schoolmaster flogged him fifteen times in one morning. Relating this latter incident, many years afterwards, he said, " We must whip children, but we must also love them."

At school he was taught the catechism, the ten commandments, the apostle's creed, the Lord's prayer, and a little Latin; but his thoughts were not directed to God, and his only religious sentiment at this time was fear. When the gentle Saviour was spoken of, he turned pale with affright; for as yet he only knew Him as an angry Judge.

John Luther wished to make his son a scholar, so, when he was fourteen years old, he was taken from the school at Mansfeld, and sent to a better one at Magdeburg, a town not very far off. His mother was sorry to part with him, but she gave her consent, and he left home to enter upon his new studies. A young friend went with him, whose name was John Reinke.

The two boys were not happy at this school. A lad of fourteen, thrown upon the world without friends or protectors, Luther trembled when in the presence of his masters, and when his studies were over he painfully begged his bread in company with children poorer than himself. One day, about Christmas time, they were wandering through the neighbouring villages singing their pretty carols on the infant Jesus. Cold and hungry, they stopped before a peasant's cottage, hoping that some kind person hearing them singing would come and give them food to eat. "Where are you boys?" cried out a harsh voice. The boys were frightened, and ran away as fast as their legs would carry them. The farmer followed; he had a harsh voice but a kind heart, and, calling them back, he gave them food, for which they were very grateful.

After being at Magdeburg about a year, his parents sent him to a grammar school at Eisenach. This they did because they had heard of the difficulty which he found in supporting himself, and as his father had relatives living in the town to which he was going, John Luther hoped these would help to support his son. They, however, took no care about him, and when pinched by hunger he had to sing and beg at Eisenach, as he had done before at Magdeburg.

Martin loved his studies, and God, who so kindly watches over us all, did not forget the friendless boy. One day, having been turned away from three houses, he was standing still, feeling very sad, before the door of a worthy citizen. Must he leave his studies, and return to labour with his father in the mines of Mansfeld? Suddenly a door opens, and a woman appears. It is Ursula, the wife of Conrad Cotta, the burgomaster of the city. She had often heard the lad's sweet voice, and remarked his attentive behaviour in church, and, seeing him standing so sad before her door, she speaks kindly to him, brings him into the house, and sets food before him. Conrad, when he came home, quite approved of what his good wife had done, and found so much pleasure in the boy's society that he took him altogether to live in his house.

Here he lived very peacefully for about five years. He was so cheerful and obliging that all who knew him loved him. He learned to play on the flute and the lute. Accompanying his fine alto voice by this latter instrument, he took special delight in testifying by his melody his gratitude towards his adoptive mother, who was very fond of music. His love for his kind protectors was very great, and it is pleasing to read that many years afterwards, when Martin Luther was the great and learned doctor of Wittemberg, he joyfully received one of their sons, who came to that city to study, into his house.

Remembering the kind Ursula, he said, "There is nothing sweeter on earth than the heart of a woman in which piety dwells." His own heart was strengthened, and his confidence in God so deeply rooted that the severest trials could not afterwards shake it.

While under Conrad's roof, the strength of his understanding, the liveliness of his imagination, and the excellence of his memory, carried him beyond all his school-fellows. He made rapid progress, especially in Latin, in eloquence, and in poetry.

> "God is our refuge in distress,
>   Our shield of hope through every care,
> Our Shepherd watching us to bless,
>   And therefore will we not despair;
>   Although the mountains shake,
>   And hills their place forsake,
>   And billows o'er them break,
>   Yet still will we not fear,
> For Thou, O God, art ever near."
>
> LUTHER.

CHAPTER II.

The Student at Erfurt.

"The fear of the Lord is the beginning of knowledge."—
PROV. i. 7.

LUTHER was now eighteen, a young man earnestly thirsting for knowledge. His father wished him to study the law, and hoped great things for his talented son. He therefore sent him to the University of Erfurt. This was in 1501.
Here he attentively studied the philosophy of the Middle Ages, and read Cicero, Virgil, and other classic authors. The whole university admired his genius; but even at this time he did not learn merely to cultivate the intellect and win worldly fame. A deeper importance began to attach itself to his studies, and those serious thoughts and that heart directed heavenwards, which God gives to those whom He purposes to make His most zealous ministers, were his. He felt his dependence upon God, and earnestly asked His blessing upon all that he engaged in. "To pray well," he said, "is the better half of study."

The Student at Erfurt.

All his spare time he spent in the library of the university;—and now a new impulse and direction were about to be given to his desires. One day, when he had been at Erfurt about two years, and was twenty years old, he was taking down book after book, looking at their authors' names. He comes to one that attracts his attention. He holds it in his hands, reads the title,—pauses; reads again,—a Bible! a rare book, unknown in those days. He opens its pages, and the story of Hannah and young Samuel is before him. His soul is full of joy as he reads it, and he returns home with the thought: "Oh, if God would give me such a book for my own!" Day after day found him in the library reading the newly discovered treasure.

At this time he twice narrowly escaped death. His severe study brought on a dangerous illness, and his friends thought that he would die. He feared so himself. To a kind old priest who visited him, he said, "Soon I shall be called away from this world;" but the old man replied, "My dear bachelor, take courage; you will not die of this illness. Our God will yet make of you a man who, in turn, shall console many."

Shortly after, he was going home to spend a short time with his parents, and, according to the custom of the age, wore a sword. The blade accidentally fell out, and cut one of his principal arteries. The blood gushed forth. His companion fled for assistance, and Luther, left alone, laid down on his back, trying in vain to stop the bleeding by pressing his finger upon the wound. Thinking death was approaching he cried, "O Mary, help me!" He then trusted in Mary; later on, his only trust was in Jesus.

Yet another event occurred to direct his thoughts to the subject of death. A dear friend, named Alexis, was assassinated. He was very much grieved, and said, "What would become of me if I were thus called away without warning?"

While his father was urging him to study the law, his heart told him that religion was the one thing needful, and his thoughts turned towards a monastic life. He felt that if he were shut out from the world he would become holy, and that the sins which troubled him so much would depart.

It is now 1505, and Luther has been made Master of Arts and Doctor of Philosophy. We see that he is becoming a learned man.

He has again paid his parents a visit, and is returning to Erfurt. When a short distance from that city a violent thunder-storm comes on. The lightning flashes, the thunder roars, the bolt seems to fall at his feet. He is greatly terrified, and falls upon his knees. Death, the judgment, eternity, are all present before him. He makes a solemn vow that if God will spare him, he will forsake the world and devote himself to religion. The storm passes away, and he rises from his knees. The sun shines out again, but darkness remains upon his heart. He feels that he must become holy; but how? As yet he knows not of the cleansing power of Jesus' blood. To become a monk is his idea of finding holiness.

He enters Erfurt again, and one evening he invites his college friends to a cheerful but frugal supper. All are happy; but while the merry talk goes on, Luther tells them of his resolve. They are sad, and entreat him not to go; but all is of no avail. That night, taking with him only a few books, he left his lodgings, went to the convent of St. Augustine, asked admittance, was received, and the talented young doctor was separated from the world. Only twenty-two, and shut out from his parents and all that he loved best on earth!

> Dying souls, fast bound in sin,
> Trembling and repining;
> With no ray of light Divine
> On your pathway shining;
> Why in darkness wander on,
> Filled with consternation?
> Jesus lives—in Him alone
> Can you find salvation.

CHAPTER III.

The Monk.

"In Him was life; and the life was the light of men."—
JOHN i. 4.

JOHN LUTHER was very angry when he heard what his son had done. All the bright hopes that he had cherished seemed overthrown through one imprudent step. It was not until two of his other sons died of the plague, and he heard it reported that Martin was dead also, that he forgave him. The friends at Erfurt were astonished. For two days they clustered round the convent, hoping to see Luther; but the gates remained closed and barred. A month passed away before they were able to speak to their late companion.

When Martin Luther entered the convent, he changed his name, and took that of Augustine.

What is the young monk doing? Is he full of joy because his sins are gone? No; sin is still there. Is he happy in following his studies? No; he must work, and not read. The monks at first treated him very harshly. He was made porter, to open and shut the gates; he had to wind up the clock, to sweep the church, and to clean the cells. When this was done, he took his bag and begged from house to house. He returns tired, and thinks now he will be able to rest and read his books, but the other monks come and roughly call him away, saying, "Come, come! it is not by studying, but by begging bread, corn, eggs, fish, meat, and money that a monk renders himself useful to the cloister."

He bore all patiently, thinking these unpleasant things were but discipline leading to holiness. At the intercession of the University he was, after a time, freed from his meaner duties, and returned to his studies. But his studies, his fasting, his sleepless nights, are wearing him away, and he becomes pale and thin. His mind is still vigorous, and frequently he may be seen in the public disputation unravelling the most complicated reasoning.

In the convent he found a Bible fastened by a chain. To this he constantly returned. He loved the Word of God, but as yet it only spoke to him of that holiness which he could not attain. He tries more earnestly, he shuts himself up in his cell, repeats his Latin prayers over and over; but his conscience troubles him, and he says to himself, "Look, thou art still envious, impatient, passionate. It profiteth thee nothing. Oh! wretched man, to have entered this sacred order!" For seven weeks he hardly slept; for four days he remained without eating or drinking. On one occasion he had shut himself up in his cell, and suffered no one to enter for several days. A friend, named Lucas Edemberger, feeling anxious about him, took with him some chorister boys, and knocked at his door. No one opens, no one answers —all is still! Much alarmed, Edemberger breaks open the door. Luther lies upon the floor apparently dead. He is worn out with fasting, want of sleep, and the unhappiness of his heart. His friend strives in vain to bring him to his senses, and it is only when he hears the sweet voices of the chorister boys singing a hymn that he returns to consciousness. His troubles caused him more attentively to study the Bible, and the time now drew near when he was to meet with a friend to whom he could tell all his sorrows.

John Staupitz, the vicar-general of the Augustine convents in Germany, was about to visit Erfurt. Though a Roman Catholic, he was a good man, who knew much of the love and mercy of Jesus, and had a kind heart. He himself had endured similar struggles to those of Luther, and had found peace in Jesus Christ. As he was making his usual inspection of the convent at Erfurt, and the monks were gathered before him, he especially noticed one,—a young man of middle height, whom study, fasting, and prolonged watchings had wasted away till all his bones could be counted. This young man was Luther; and Staupitz, quickly seeing what was passing within, very kindly approached him, and succeeded in gaining his confidence. He showed him how useless it was to trust in good works for salvation, and explained the way in which God pardons sin through faith in

Jesus; he also told him how foolish it was to wait for repentance before he believed in the loving kindness of God. "If you desire to be converted," said he, "do not be anxious about these mortifications, and all these tortures. Love Him who first loved you!' Staupitz did more than this; for, on leaving the convent, he gave Luther a Bible, and besought him to let the study of the Scriptures be his favourite occupation.

Never was advice better taken and obeyed. The dark clouds were now rolling away, and happiness began to dawn upon the young monk; but the mists had not quite dispersed. The good seed had been sown in his heart, but there yet remained much for him to learn.

He was again laid aside by sickness, and appeared to be dying. His anxieties and fears returned, and he was sinking into despair. An old monk entered his cell, and kindly spoke to him. Luther told him of his misery and fear. The old man could not counsel like Staupitz, but he knew his creed, and it had comforted his heart. Simply he repeated, "I believe in the forgiveness of sins." The sick man slowly said the words, "I believe in the forgiveness of sins." "Ah!" exclaimed the aged brother, "you must believe not only in the forgiveness of David's and Peter's sins, but you must believe that your own sins are forgiven." "Hear also what St. Bernard says," said he: "'The testimony in thy heart is this: thy sins are forgiven thee.'"

From this moment Luther had peace, and could

say with St. Paul, " Being justified by faith, we have peace with God through our Lord Jesus Christ." He realised also the power of the Saviour's words, " Peace I leave with you ; my peace I give unto you : not as the world giveth, give I unto you."

> Jesus, Thou art my righteousness,
>   For all my sins were Thine ;
> Thy death hath bought of God my peace
>   Thy life hath made Him mine.
> Spotless and just in Thee I am ;
>   I feel my sins forgiven :
> I taste salvation in Thy name,
>   And antedate my heaven.

CHAPTER IV.

Luther at Wittemberg.

"With joy shall ye draw water out of the wells of salvation."—Isa. xii. 3.

LUTHER had been a monk nearly two years when, on the 2nd May, 1507, he was ordained a priest. He had invited his father to be present at the ceremony, and had asked him to fix the day. John Luther accepted the invitation, and showed his affection and generosity by presenting the young priest with twenty florins.

After the ordination, John dined at the convent with his son and the other Augustine monks. The conversation turned to the subject of Luther's entering the monastery. The monks praised him greatly for so doing; but the father, turning to his son, said, "Have you not read in Scripture that you should obey your father and mother?" These words sank deeply into Luther's heart.

New scenes were now about to open out before the young priest, and a different, but more congenial position was to be assigned to him.

Staupitz, who had not forgotten the young monk, but corresponded frequently with him, spoke of him to Frederick, the good and wise Elector of Saxony, who invited him to become professor at the University of Wittemberg. This was in 1508.

Upon his arrival at Wittemberg he went to the Augustine convent, where a cell was prepared for him; for though now a professor, he still remained a monk. He zealously entered upon his new duties, and was appointed to teach a great many learned and difficult subjects. But his desire was for the Bible,—for time to study it himself, and for opportunity to teach it to others. He continued the study of Greek and Hebrew, so that he might be able to read the Scriptures in their original languages. A few months after this, having obtained the degree of Bachelor of Divinity, he was called upon to lecture on the Bible every day at one o'clock.

Luther was now engaged in a work that he loved. The Word of God became more and more precious to him, and he delighted to impart its truths to his pupils. While studying for one of his lectures, the first chapter of Romans, a bright light seemed to shine upon the seventeenth verse, "The just shall live by faith." This text had a great influence in moulding the character of the reformer.

Staupitz rejoiced in the talents of his friend, and, wishing him to be still more useful, asked him to preach in the Church of the Augustines. "No, no!" he replied, "it is no slight thing to speak

Luther at Wittemberg.

before men in the place of God." Staupitz persevered, and at last Luther yielded.

In the middle of the Square at Wittemberg stood an old wooden chapel, thirty feet long and twenty wide. Its walls were propped up on all sides, and an old pulpit, made of planks, three feet high, received the preacher. In this humble place the preaching of the Reformation began.

The minds of the people at this time were very dark. God's Word was unknown. Ignorance and superstition prevailed. They worshipped old bones, which they were told had been parts of the bodies of holy men, bits of wood, and other relics. They heard prayers in Latin, and bowed down at the mass. If they did wrong they went to a priest, confessed, and did penance; or else procured an indulgence. They believed in a dreadful purgatory, in whose flames the souls of the departed must be tortured until satisfaction had been made for their crimes. The bishops and priests were too often bad men, and gained money by picturing the dreadful sufferings of those in purgatory; telling the people that if they paid money the poor tortured souls of those they loved would be liberated sooner. Truly darkness covered the land, and gross darkness the people.

Luther preached. He was still a Papist, but he was drawing truth from the Bible. Everything in the new minister was striking. His clear voice, his noble air, his expressive countenance, charmed his hearers; while the deep seriousness of his manner, and the joy that evidently filled his heart, when he spoke of the love of Christ for sinners, gave to his eloquence an authority and a warmth which deeply impressed his hearers.

His fame spread far and wide, the little chapel could not contain the crowds that flocked to it, and Luther was asked to preach in the parish church. Frederick the Elector once came to Wittemberg to hear him.

> In a service which Thy love appoints,
>   There are no bonds for me :
> For my secret heart is taught the tru h
>   That makes Thy people free ;
> And a life of self-renouncing love,
>   Is a life of liberty.

CHAPTER V.

The Visit to Rome.

"Having a form of godliness, but denying the power thereof: from such turn away."—2 TIM. iii. 5.

LUTHER imagined Rome to be a most holy city. It was necessary for him to see it, and he visited it in 1510.

There was a difference of opinion between Staupitz and seven of the Augustine convents, and Luther was chosen to lay the matter before the Pope.

He set out, and crossed the Alps, and descended into the plains of Italy. At every step he found subjects of astonishment and scandal. He was entertained in a wealthy Italian convent of the Benedictines. When he saw the splendid apartments, the rich dresses, and the delicate food, he was confounded. Marble, silk, luxury in all its forms—what a sight for the humble brother of the poor convent of Wittemberg! Friday came—a fast day with Roman Catholics,—but Luther saw the table covered with meat. He was shocked, and resolved to speak. "The Church and the Pope," said he, "forbid such things." The Benedictines were very angry, and the porter of the convent warned him that it would be dangerous to make a longer stay. He quitted this wealthy convent, and went on to Bologna, where he fell dangerously ill.

Recovered from his sickness, he proceeded onward, and, after a toilsome journey under a burning Italian sun, he at length saw the seven-hilled city in the distance. Falling on his knees, he exclaimed: "Holy Rome, I salute thee!" But when he entered the city and saw the great wickedness which abounded on every hand, he felt that it was far from holy. He saw that the priests and high dignitaries of the Church only made a mock of religion, or else performed their duties with indecent haste and in a mechanical manner. On one occasion he was engaged in celebrating mass, when he found that the priests at an adjoining altar had repeated seven masses before he had finished one. Growing impatient, a priest cried out to him, "Make haste, make haste; have done with it quickly."

Luther went to Rome a devout Papist, and at first gave himself up to all the vain superstitions of the Church. He visited the churches and chapels, he believed the falsehoods that were told him, he knelt before the shrines of the saints,—he even wished that his parents were dead, so that by his good works he might have the pleasure of delivering their souls from purgatory. One day, wishing to obtain an indulgence, which the Pope had promised to all who should ascend on their knees what is called Pilate's Staircase, he began slowly to crawl up those steps, when a voice like thunder seemed to speak from the bottom of his heart, "The just shall live by faith." He started from his knees, and rushed from the spot ashamed of his superstitious folly.

Luther went to Rome, believing that city to be the most holy spot upon earth; he left it with the conviction, expressed in his own words: "No one can imagine what sins and infamous actions are committed in Rome; they must be seen and heard to be believed. Thus they are in the habit of saying, 'If there be a hell, Rome is built over it'; it is an abyss whence issues every kind of sin."

This visit was of great importance to Luther, and he afterwards said, "If they would give me one hundred thousand florins I would not have missed seeing Rome."

Having finished the business entrusted to him, he returned to Wittemberg.

The preaching of the young professor had made a deep impression on the Elector, and that prince, and also Staupitz, wished to advance him to yet higher honours. He was therefore made Doctor of Divinity, the Elector generously agreeing to pay all expenses. This was on 19th October, 1512. He then solemnly promised to preach the Holy Scriptures faithfully, to teach them with purity, to study them all his life, and to defend them, both in disputation and in writing, against all false teachers, so far as God should give him ability.

Nobly Luther kept his vow, and not only in the

University classes, or in the church, did he preach the Gospel, but among his private friends he was always anxious to lead them to trust in Jesus and Him crucified.

About this time he became acquainted with George Spalatin, secretary and chaplain to the Elector, a man of great worth, to whom Luther became much attached. Through his hands passed all the business between the reformer and the Elector.

In 1516, Staupitz was sent by Frederick into the Low Countries to collect relics; and Luther was appointed to take his place during his absence, and in particular to visit the convents in his stead.

Amongst others, he came to the monastery at Erfurt where he had once wound up the clock, opened the gates, and swept out the church. He was now visiting it as the vicar-general, and we know that he tried to comfort many hearts. He urged the monks to lay aside their books of philosophy and to study the Word of God. Many of the Augustine monks afterwards became faithful preachers of the Gospel, and so much good followed from this journey that the year in which it took place has been called "the morning star of the Reformation." He returned to Wittemberg after an absence of about six weeks.

About this time the plague broke out in that town. Many fled, but Luther remained. "You advise me to flee," he wrote to a friend: "whither shall I flee? If the pestilence spreads, I shall disperse the brothers in every direction; but as for me, my place is here; duty does not permit me to desert my post until He who has called me shall summon me away. Not that I have no fear of death, but I hope that the Lord will deliver me from fear."

Such was the brave and faithful man who was to attack the giant power of Rome with the sword of the Spirit, the Word of God. As yet he was full of respect for the Pope and the Romish religion.

Staupitz returned with a valuable supply of relics, and the Elector, greatly pleased, thought to make him a bishop. Luther, who was bold in the presence of the terrible plague, was also bold before the mighty of this world. He wrote to Spalatin telling him that it was wrong, and saying, "There are many things which please your prince, and which nevertheless are displeasing to God."

In July, 1517, he preached before Duke George of Saxony, in whose States Dresden and Leipsic were situated. The sermon gave great offence to the Duke and his Court, but was made a blessing to a lady of high rank, who, a month afterwards, died trusting in Jesus.

> O Christ ! He is the fountain,
>   The deep, sweet well of love ;
> The streams on earth I've tasted,
>   More deep I'll drink above ;
> There to an ocean fulness,
>   His mercy doth expand,
> And glory—glory dwelleth
>   In Emmanuel's land.

CHAPTER VI.

The Indulgences.

"I, even I, am He that blotteth out thy transgressions for mine own sake, and will not remember thy sins."—Isa. xliii. 25.

A GREAT agitation now prevailed in Germany. Pope Leo X. wanted money to meet the lavish expenditure of his Court, and the expense incurred by the building of St. Peter's Church. He issued a bull, or edict, declaring a general indulgence,— to be paid for by those who received it,—the proceeds of which were to be appropriated to the building of St. Peter's.

The sale of these indulgences caused great scandal in Germany. The sins of the Germans, as they were called, had been farmed to Albert, the Archbishop and Elector of Mentz; and the agent employed by him was a Dominican monk, John Tetzel, a bad man, whom the Emperor Maximilian, on one occasion, ordered to be put into a sack and thrown into the river on account of his crimes.

Tetzel was forbidden to enter the dominions of

The Indulgences.

Frederick the Elector; he came as near as he could, and established himself at Juterbuch, four miles from Wittemberg.

A grand procession is advancing! The whole of the people are in motion! Amidst the clouds of dust see a handsome carriage, accompanied by three horsemen. The clergy, priests, and nuns, carrying lighted tapers; the council; the schoolmasters and their pupils; the trades with their banners; men and women, young and old, all go out to meet it; and, while music is playing and bells ringing, they follow it to the church.

The Pope's bull is carried on a velvet cushion, or on cloth of gold, in front of the procession. Next follows Tetzel, robed in a Dominican's dress, moving along with an arrogant air, and bearing in his hands a large red cross. The rest follow.

Arrived at the church, the cross is placed in front of the altar, the Pope's arms are hung upon it, and daily the clergy of the place, and others, come to pay it homage.

The church is crowded, the large red cross stands before the altar. Tetzel—a strong old man of sixty-three—is in the pulpit. He has come to sell God's pardon for sin. In a loud voice he begins to extol his wares. "Indulgences," says he, "are the most precious of God's gifts. Come, and I will give you letters, all properly sealed, by which even the sins that you intend to commit may be pardoned. There is no sin so great that an indulgence cannot remit; only pay well, and all will be forgiven." He passes to another subject. "But more than this," he says; "indulgences avail not only for the living, but for the dead. For that repentance is not even necessary. Priest, noble, merchant, wife, youth, maiden! do you not hear your parents and your friends who are dead crying out to you: 'We are suffering horrible torments; a little money will deliver us; you can give it, and you will not!'" All shuddered at these words, uttered by the thundering voice of the impostor monk. "At the very instant that the money rattles at the bottom of the chest the soul escapes from purgatory, and flies liberated to heaven."

There was a money-box near, and as the monk spoke, people dropped in their coins. His speech ended, he ran towards the box, and in the sight of all flung in a piece of money, taking care that it should rattle loudly. And now the sale began; crowds came with their money to buy the indulgences which assured them of the pardon of their sins, and of permission to sin again.

How awful was it for any man to offer to sell for money that pardon which Jesus Christ purchased by His blood; or to give permission to sin, when God says: "The soul that sinneth it shall die"!

Tetzel had a regular price for different sins. To the poor his charge for murder was eight ducats, while for sacrilege and perjury he charged nine.

With all his cunning, sometimes Tetzel got taken in. On one occasion a Saxon nobleman, who had heard him at Leipsic, and was much displeased with his falsehoods, came and asked him if he had the power of pardoning sins that men intended to commit. "Most assuredly," replied he, "I have received full power from His Holiness for that purpose." "Well, then," answered the knight, "I am desirous of taking a slight revenge on one of my enemies, without endangering his life. I will give you ten crowns if you will give me a letter of indulgence that will fully justify me." Tetzel made some objection, but they came to an arrangement for thirty crowns. The monk quitted Leipsic shortly after. The nobleman and his attendants watched for him in a wood. They fell upon him and gave him a slight beating, taking from him the well-filled indulgence chest which he was carrying. Tetzel was in a furious rage; but the nobleman showed the letter of indulgence, and Duke George ordered him to be acquitted.

One upon whom Tetzel's proceedings made the deepest impression was the youthful Myconius, afterwards celebrated as a reformer and historian of the Reformation.

Luther appears to have first heard of Tetzel at Grimma, in 1516. Hearing some of his extravagant expressions quoted, he said: "If God permit, I will make a hole in his drum."

One day Luther was, as a priest, hearing his people confess their sins. Many acknowledged themselves guilty of great crimes. He rebuked them, and tried to make them lead better lives; but shocked and indignant was he when they replied that they would not abandon their sins, and that they need not, for they had bought indulgences of Tetzel. He refused to absolve them, and said, "Except ye repent, ye shall all likewise perish;" adding, "Have a care how you listen to the clamours of these indulgence merchants; you have better things to do than buy their licenses which they sell at so vile a price."

When Tetzel heard of this he bellowed with rage, and had a fire lighted in the market-place, declaring that he had received an order from the Pope to burn all heretics who presumed to oppose his holy indulgences.

Luther, nothing daunted, ascended the pulpit of his church and preached boldly against them. This he did notwithstanding the fact that special indulgences had been granted by the Pope for the Elector's castle-chapel at Wittemberg.

The sermon was printed, and made a profound impression on all who read it.

> My hope is built on nothing less
> Than Jesu's blood and righteousness;
> I dare not trust the sweetest frame,
> But wholly lean on Jesu's name;
> On Christ the solid rock I stand;
> All other ground is sinking sand.

CHAPTER VII.

The Theses.

"Who can forgive sins, but God alone?"—LUKE v. 21.

LUTHER prepared for a yet bolder step. He has warned his people in the confessional, he has preached from the pulpit to his congregation; he will now speak as a theologian, addressing all those who, like himself, are teachers of the Word of God. The feast of All Saints drew near, a very important day at Wittemberg, especially for the church which Frederick had built and filled with relics. On this day these relics, ornamented with gold, silver, and precious stones, were exhibited to the people, and whoever then visited the church, and made confession, obtained a rich indulgence.

On the day preceding the festival, 31st October, 1517, Luther walked boldly towards the church, and in the presence of all who were assembled, affixed to the church-door a paper containing ninety-five short sentences, called theses, against the doctrine of indulgences. Three of them were as follows:—

"They preach mere human follies who maintain that as soon as the money rattles in the strong box the soul flies out of purgatory." "They are the enemies of the Pope and of Jesus Christ, who, by reason of the preaching of indulgences, forbid the preaching of the Word of God." "The indulgence of the Pope cannot take away the smallest daily sin, as far as regards the guilt or the offence."

Great was the attention excited. The Theses were read and spoken of on all sides. In a fortnight they were in every part of Germany, and in a month they had found their way to Rome. Somewhat later they were translated into Dutch and Spanish, and a traveller sold them in Jerusalem. Many were delighted with them, and monks in their cells, and peasants in their cottages, rejoiced that they had heard the voice of truth. The Emperor Maximilian read them, and wrote to the Elector of Saxony, "Take great care of the monk Luther, for the time may come when we shall have need of him." Even the Pope was more amused than angry, and when urged to burn him as a heretic, replied, " Brother Martin Luther is a very fine genius, and all that is said against him is mere monkish jealousy"

But some were fearful of the results that would follow. The Elector was uneasy, and the principal men of Luther's own convent were alarmed. They came to his cell trembling, and besought him not to bring disgrace upon their order. He nobly replied, "Dear fathers, if this work be not of God, it will come to nought; but if it be, let it go forward."

The Theses.

Tetzel prepared some theses in reply to those of Luther. Not content with this, he stated his hope and belief that the heretic would be burnt; and as a sign he caused the reformer's Theses to be cast into the flames,—an act which was afterwards repaid by the students of Wittemberg, who burnt his own theses in the market-place of that town.

Luther was much grieved when he heard of this revenge having been taken. He wished for peace and order, and always maintained that the cause of God was not to be advanced by any recourse to force or arms.

About this time he published his sermons on the Ten Commandments and his "Explanation of the Lord's Prayer;" these works being issued with the object of carrying the truth to the homes of the people.

The contest continued. The Dominicans were especially fierce in their assault. The Bishop of Brandenburg said, "I will not lay my head down in peace until I have thrown Martin into the fire like this brand," and he threw a piece of wood into the fire. But the most violent in his attack was one who had been a friend, Dr. Eck, of Ingolstadt. Luther wrote him a letter full of affection, but to this he received no reply. Rome now began to take part in the combat; Prierio, the Roman censor, attacked the reformer's Theses, employing by turns ridicule, insults, and menaces.

In the spring of 1518, Luther was called to take part in an important meeting of the Augustine order, held at Heidelberg. Here he defended some theses which he had written so ably that he won much applause; but, better still, he was the means of bringing many to see the light—one of whom was Bucer, who afterwards wrote many good books, which were made a great blessing to England.

On his return from Heidelberg, Luther wrote an explanation of his Theses, firmly upholding the truth, but softening down some passages that had given offence. He sent this book, which he called "Resolutions," to the Pope through his friend Staupitz, with a letter full of humility, respect, and submission.

Luther wished for peace, and supposed that Leo X. was a just man and a sincere lover of the truth. In this we shall see that he was mistaken.

But while he was looking to the Pope for justice, Rome was meditating plans of vengeance against him. The first effort made was to draw away the powerful support of the Elector, but this failed. The next step was to cite him to Rome. The Emperor Maximilian had written a letter to the Pope concerning the reformer, in which he said, "We will take care that whatever your Holiness may decree in this matter for the glory of God shall be enforced throughout the empire;" and Leo X. began to consider it was time to put forth his strength and to crush the poor Augustine monk who had dared to preach against his indulgences.

Having sent his letter to the Pope, Luther left the

matter in the hands of God, and quietly awaited the result. Two days, however, only had elapsed when he received a summons to appear at Rome to answer charges made against him.

"At the very moment I was expecting a blessing," said he, "I saw the thunderbolt fall upon me. I was the lamb that troubled the water the wolf was drinking. Tetzel escaped, and I was to permit myself to be devoured."

His friends were filled with alarm. If he went to Rome, he went, as they saw, to certain death, while if he refused to appear he would be condemned for disrespect of the Pope's authority. Luther felt that only the Elector could save him, but he was unwilling to involve his kind prince in trouble. The University of Wittemberg wrote a letter of entreaty to the Pope, and also to his chamberlain, Charles Miltitz. They said, "The weakness of Luther's frame and the dangers of the journey render it difficult, and even impossible, for him to obey the order of your Holiness." The Elector also wrote to the Emperor concerning him.

Finally it was arranged that the reformer should appear in Augsburg, a German city, instead of at Rome; and the Pope ordered his legate, Cardinal Cajetan—otherwise known as De Vio—to try the matter there. This was not done by the Pope out of any compassion for Luther. His writ was cruel, and authorised the legate to prosecute the Wittemberg doctor without delay, to invoke the aid of the Emperor and princes of Germany, to keep the reformer in safe custody, and to excommunicate all those who adhered to his cause. He was proceeded against by the Bishop of Ascoli, and declared a heretic, unheard.

Luther was at this time much cheered by the arrival at Wittemberg of a young man of great ability and much gentleness. It was Philip Melancthon, who became a very dear friend, and was destined to take a leading part with him in the work of the Reformation. Melancthon had been invited by the Elector to become professor of ancient languages at the University of Wittemberg. He was then twenty-one years of age.

The Pope wrote a very flattering letter to the Elector, in which he urged him to watch over the honour of his name, and to deliver Luther into the legate's hands. The good Elector did not yield, but sent him letters of recommendation to some of the principal councillors of Augsburg, and furnished him with money for his journey.

The citation to Rome having been changed to a summons to appear at Augsburg, Luther resolved to obey it, although entreated by many of his friends not to do so, and informed that several powerful lords had determined to either strangle or drown him on his way thither. Staupitz was much alarmed, and wrote begging Martin to come and live with him, so that both might live and die together.

But Luther feared nothing but sinning against God; and the words of Scripture continually sounded in his ears, " Whosoever shall confess me before men, him will I also confess before my father which is in heaven."

> Soon, and for ever ! the work shall be done,
> The warfare accomplished, the victory won ;
> Soon, and for ever ! the soldier lay down
> His sword for a harp, and his cross for a crown ;
> Then droop not in sorrow, despond not in fear,
> A glorious to-morrow is brightening and near.

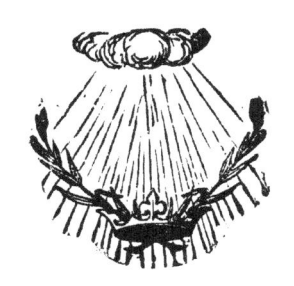

CHAPTER VIII

Augsburg.

"Our soul is escaped as a bird out of the snare of the fowlers: the snare is broken, and we are escaped."—Ps. cxxiv. 7.

WE have seen Luther contending with Tetzel, we have witnessed him defending his Theses in the presence of learned doctors; we are now about to see him brought face to face with the power of Rome itself.

Having received the letters of recommendation sent him by the Elector, he quietly set out on foot for Augsburg. He must have felt sad as he left his much-loved Wittemberg to appear before the Roman legate, and without a safe-conduct. Death may be very near, but he advanced without fear to bear his testimony to the Gospel.

On the 28th September he reached Weimar, where the Elector was holding his Court. Here he preached. He next stopped at Nuremberg, where, as his own dress was old, he borrowed a frock from his friend Wenceslas Link, the preacher there, so that he might appear in a becoming dress before the prince of the Roman Church. From this town Link and a monk named Leonard accompanied him.

When within five leagues of Augsburg, Luther was taken so ill that he thought he was going to die. His friends procured a waggon, in which they placed him, and in this condition he entered the city on Friday, 7th October, 1518.

He took up his abode at the convent of the Augustines, where he soon recovered.

His first business was to send Link to the Cardinal to announce his arrival.

The next morning, while thinking upon his peculiar position, he was informed that a stranger was about to visit him. Shortly after, a cunning Italian courtier, Serra Longa, appeared, and in a most plausible manner tried to get Luther to retract. He came as a friend, but he was sent as a spy by the Cardinal. Failing in this, he went away. Meanwhile the councillors to whom the Elector had recommended Luther strongly urged him not to go before the legate without a safe-conduct, which they offered to procure.

Serra Longa returned, and stated that the Cardinal was waiting. Luther informed him of the advice of his Augsburg friends, and refused to proceed until the safe-conduct arrived.

In acting thus, Luther well knew that a safe-conduct had not saved John Huss from being burnt; and he only insisted upon having one in compliance with the wishes of those to whom the Elector had entrusted him.

On the Monday following, the safe-conduct arrived, and Cajetan was informed that Luther would wait upon him on the morrow.

Shortly before the arrival of the safe-conduct, Serra Longa again appeared. "Why do you not wait upon the Cardinal?" he said; "he is expecting you most indulgently. The whole matter lies in six letters— *r-e-v-o-c-a*—retract. Come, you have nothing to fear." Luther thought these six letters very important ones, but he told him that he was waiting for the safe-conduct, when he would immediately appear before Cajetan.

Serra Longa grew very angry, and, after accusing Luther of imagining that the Elector would take up arms in his defence, said, "When all forsake you, where will you take refuge?"

Luther (looking upwards).—"Under heaven."

Serra Longa.—"What would you do if you held the legate, Pope, and cardinals in your hands, as they have you now in theirs?"

Luther.—"I would show them all possible honour and respect, but with me the Word of God is before everything."

Such was the sturdy man whom Rome thought to conquer. His strength was in the Lord of Hosts, and his weapon the Sword of the Spirit—the Word of God.

Accompanied by a few friends, Luther, on Tuesday, the 11th October, went to the palace of the legate. Crowds pressed upon him as he went along. Cajetan received him with coldness but civility. When the salutations were over, Luther stated "that he appeared in obedience to the summons of the Pope and the orders of the Elector of Saxony; that he acknowledged the propositions and theses ascribed to him; that he was ready to listen to his accusation; and, if he had erred, to receive instruction in the truth."

But Cajetan had not received instructions to argue with the reformer. At first he spoke kindly, saying, "My dear son," and pointing out two propositions, he requested that Luther would retract them. Finding him firm, he grew angry, and said, "I did not come here to dispute with you. Retract, or prepare to suffer the penalty you have deserved."

Having refused a safe-conduct to appear at Rome, the reformer withdrew.

A very pleasant surprise awaited him upon his arrival at the convent. His old friend Staupitz, unable to prevent his appearance at Augsburg, had journeyed thither to offer him his services in this time of trial. Great was Luther's joy when he beheld his friend.

By the advice of Staupitz, the reformer determined to answer the Cardinal in writing.

Accordingly, taking with him a public notary, he, the next day, again repaired to the legate's palace, and in the presence of all assembled read the declaration which he had prepared. In this he stated his willingness to receive instruction, but protested against being compelled to retract without having been refuted.

Cajetan would hear nothing but the words, "I retract"; and turning to the two propositions, he overwhelmed the doctor with objections, allowing him no opportunity of replying.

Luther, and Staupitz, who had accompanied him, saw the hopelessness of attempting to either enlighten the Cardinal or to make any useful confession of faith. The reformer, therefore, begged leave to transmit his answer in writing; and this request being supported by his friends, was granted. The second interview had ended as unsatisfactorily as the first.

On Friday, the 14th, he returned to the Cardinal for the third and last time. The Italians, who formed the train of this prince of the Church, crowded round him as usual. He advanced and presented the protest that he had written. Cajetan glanced at it, and threw the paper aside with contempt, declaring that Luther ought to retract. The interview ended in threatenings. The legate, having been confounded upon a point on which he laid special stress, cried out, "Retract! retract! or, if you do not, I shall send you to Rome. I shall excommunicate you with all your partisans, with all who are or may be favourable to you, and reject them from the Church."

"Deign," replied Luther, "to forward to Pope Leo X., with my humble prayers, the answer which I have handed you in writing."

Cajetan answered with pride and anger, " Retract, or return no more."

Luther marked the words and withdrew, followed

Augsburg.

by the councillors of the Elector. He and Cajetan never met again, but the reformer had made an impression on the legate which was never entirely effaced.

Later in the day the Cardinal sent for Staupitz and Wenceslas Link, and urged upon them the necessity of persuading Luther to retract; but this they declared was beyond their power. He then stated that he would send to the reformer in writing what it was required that he should retract.

Saturday and Sunday passed without any writing coming from Cajetan, and Luther's friends began to be much alarmed. "The legate," said they, "is preparing some mischief, and it is very much to be feared that you will all be seized and cast into prison."

On Monday, Luther wrote to the Cardinal, but received no reply to his letter. Fearing this stillness on the part of the legate and his courtiers boded no good, those to whom the reformer had been confided urged him to draw up an appeal to the Pope, and to quit Augsburg without delay,—Staupitz, Link, and the Elector's councillors had already left.

Having now waited four days in the city uselessly, he determined to leave; but before doing so he wrote a second letter to the Cardinal, which was to be given to that prelate after the reformer's departure. He also drew up an appeal to the Pope, to be posted upon the cathedral gates two or three days after he had left.

On Wednesday, before daylight, a pony which

Staupitz had left for him was brought to the door of the convent. Luther bids his brethren farewell. Without a bridle for his horse, without boots or spurs, and unarmed, he sets off. A guide has been provided who conducts him in silence through the streets. They make their way to a small gate in the walls of the city, which has purposely been left open,—they pass through, and soon the poor, but noble-minded monk, who has dared to oppose the haughty power of Rome, is galloping away far from the walls of Augsburg.

> When exposed to fearful dangers,
>   Jesus will his own defend;
> Borne afar, midst foes and strangers,
>   Jesus will appear your friend;
> And His presence
>   Shall be with you to the end.

CHAPTER IX.

A Truce.

"Behold, God is my salvation; I will trust, and not be afraid."—ISA. xii. 2.

CAJETAN was exceedingly mortified when he heard of Luther's escape. He was thunderstruck, and even frightened and alarmed. He had done nothing; he had neither humbled Luther nor punished him. He wrote a letter to the Elector desiring that prince either to send the reformer to Rome, or to banish him from his dominions; adding a postscript in his own writing entreating Frederick "not to tarnish his honour and that of his illustrious ancestors for the sake of a miserable little friar."

The Elector refused either to send Luther to Rome or to banish him from his States. But although secure in the Elector's favour, he felt that he might be compelled to leave Germany, and he looked to France as the country where he might hope to have the opportunity of announcing the truth without fear of opposition.

The hour of his departure indeed seemed at hand. He had written to the Elector begging that he might not be sent to Rome, but offering to resign himself to banishment. He had preached a farewell sermon to his congregation, and now he waits in humble trust the will of Him without whose knowledge not a sparrow falls to the ground.

The prince informs Luther that he desires him to leave Wittemberg. A farewell repast is provided. His friends are once more seated around him. He enjoys their sweet conversation, their tender and anxious friendship. A knock comes; a letter arrives! The Elector inquires why he delays so long. He is sad, but a bright ray of comfort comes. He lifts up his head and joyfully exclaims, as he looks on those around him, "Father and mother abandon me, but the Lord takes me up." Tears roll down the cheeks of his friends. Another messenger; a second letter! Everything is changed. "Since the Pope's new envoy hopes that all may be arranged by a conference, remain for the present." So wrote the Elector.

Luther now published his report of the Augsburg Conference, and on the 28th November, 1518, in the chapel of Corpus Christi at Wittemberg, he appealed from the Pope to a General Council of the Church. This was a bold step. A former Pope had pronounced the greater excommunication, even against the emperors who should be guilty of such an act of revolt.

But an event now happened which partly diverted the attention of the Pope from the German reformer.

A Truce.

On the 12th January, 1519, the Emperor Maximilian of Germany died, and Frederick of Saxony became the administrator of the empire. He was, therefore, enabled more powerfully to protect Luther, and to disregard the projects of papal nuncios.

The Pope was also so much engaged in his plans concerning the election of a new emperor, that the contest about indulgences seemed of comparatively small importance.

The new papal nuncio, Charles Miltitz, arrived in Saxony about this time. Having been informed of the scandalous proceedings of Tetzel, he became very angry, summoned that monk before him, and, upon his refusing to appear, went to Dresden where he was, and so overwhelmed him with reproaches that he was driven to despair, and soon afterwards died. Before his death, Luther, who pitied his old and bitter enemy, wrote him a letter full of kindness and consolation.

Miltitz thought that Cajetan had been too hasty in dealing with Luther, and therefore he tried flattery. They met in the house of Spalatin at Altenburg. "Do you know," said Miltitz, addressing the reformer, "that you have drawn away all the world from the Pope; even if I had an army of 25,000 men I do not think that I should be able to carry you to Rome." He had with him seventy briefs to be used for carrying him thither if the Elector delivered the reformer into his hands.

After preparing the way, as he thought, he cautiously hinted at a retractation; but Luther was determined not to retract unless it was proved that he was in error. He acknowledged that he might have spoken too violently sometimes; "But," said he, "as for a retractation, never expect one from me."

At the close of the conference, a truce was signed, both parties agreeing that they should in future neither preach, write, nor do anything further in the discussion that had been raised.

Luther was at this time full of respect for the Church of Rome, and, in his desire for peace, went so far as to write a letter to the Pope, concluding with these words: "I confess that nothing in heaven or in earth should be preferred above the Church of Rome, except Jesus Christ alone, the Lord of all."

Strange words to our ears; but in Luther's case light slowly came out of darkness. He afterwards affirmed "that it is not necessary to salvation that we should believe the Roman Church superior to others."

During the pause which now ensued in the strife, the reformer employed himself in studying the decretals of the Popes. The work of the Reformation also progressed, and the writings of the Wittemberg professor were scattered over France, the Low Countries, Italy, Spain, England, and Switzerland, everywhere creating the greatest sensation. The truce agreed to was, however, soon broken, and the combat was renewed.

Dr. Eck commenced the strife, and the famous Leipsic discussion, which lasted seventeen days, was the immediate cause of setting in motion those powers which had for a short space lain dormant.

During this disputation, in which the subjects of

the free-will of man, the supremacy of the Pope, and the doctrines of indulgences, purgatory, repentance, absolution of the priest, and satisfaction were discussed, it was seen that, however formidable was the reasoning of Eck—who was one of the most experienced schoolmen of his age,—yet that truth lay on the side of the reformer, and that the other had to resort to subtle and fallacious reasoning to meet the powerful arguments of his opponent, drawn from the Word of God.

Luther thought that much time had been wasted without any seeking after truth; but good had been done. The truth had sunk into some hearts: and Dr. Eck's secretary, Poliander; John Callarius, a celebrated Hebrew professor; and Philip Melancthon, the theologian of the Reformation, dated their conversion from this period. Luther himself was brought to see the utter fallacy of the papal pretensions to supremacy.

From this time Eck became the reformer's bitterest enemy; and early in the following year, 1520, he set out for Rome, intending to rouse the papacy to crush his powerful rival.

Luther continued to advance. About this time he published his first Commentary on the Galatians. He also questioned the authority of the Popes to canonise saints, and was led to see that the Lord's Supper was not present in the mass.

> He leadeth me, oh blessed thought!
> The words with heavenly comfort fraught:
> Whate'er I do, where'er I be,
> Still 'tis God's hand that leadeth me.

CHAPTER X.

The Papal Bull.

"Be strong and of a good courage, fear not, nor be afraid of them: for the Lord thy God, He it is that doth go with thee; He will not fail thee, nor forsake thee."—DEUT. xxxi. 6.

THE year 1520 opened. Maximilian was dead, and a new emperor had to be chosen. A new actor was about to appear upon the scene.

The imperial crown had been offered to the Elector Frederick, but that prince in his modesty declined it. The election fell upon Charles, who already possessed sovereign authority over the two Spains, Naples, Sicily, and Austria. As Charles V. he was crowned Emperor of Germany, with unusual pomp and magnificence, at Aix-la-Chapelle. The date was the 22nd October, 1520.

Luther, seeing that the cause of the Reformation would soon be carried before the new emperor, wrote to him before he left Madrid; but the young monarch took no notice of his letter.

His life was now in great danger. Fanaticism was kindled in Germany. "Now is the time," wrote he, "when men will think they do Christ service by putting us to death." One day as he was in front of the Augustine convent, a stranger, who held a pistol concealed under his cloak, accosted him, saying, "Why do you go thus alone?" "I am in God's hands," replied Luther; "He is my strength and my shield. What can man do unto me?" The stranger turned pale and fled away trembling.

Serra Longa wrote to the Elector: "Let not Luther find an asylum in the States of your Highness; let him be rejected of all, and stoned in the face of heaven; that will be more pleasing to me than if I received ten thousand crowns from you."

The storm was gathering over his head, but more especially in the direction of Rome was it expected to burst. But while the distant murmurs of the storm might be heard, God aroused the German nobles to form a bulwark for His servant. Sylvester Schaumburg, one of the most powerful knights of Franconia, sent his son with a letter for the reformer. "Your life is in danger," wrote he. "If the support of the electors, princes, or magistrates fail you, I entreat you to beware of going to Bohemia, where in former times learned men have had much to undergo; rather come to me. God willing, I shall soon have collected more than a hundred gentlemen, and with their help I shall be able to protect you, from every danger."

Letters of sympathy also reached him from many noble-minded men of that age.

When Luther received these letters he exclaimed,

"The Lord reigns, I see Him there, as if I could touch Him."

At this time the writings of the reformer were read and his words treasured in cottages and convents, in the homes of the citizens and in the castles of the nobles, in the universities and in the palaces of kings. He now issued his famous "Appeal to His Imperial Majesty, and to the Nobility of the German Nation, on the Reformation of Christianity." In this he boldly condemned the false doctrines and bad practises of the Romish Church, and even went so far as to speak of the Pope as Antichrist. In a short time over 4000 copies were sold.

The storm has burst. The Pope has issued a bull. Luther is given sixty days to forward his recantation. Failing to do this, he is condemned, with all his adherents, as open and obstinate heretics.

Dr. Eck rejoiced, and was bringing the bull into Germany. Little encouragement was given to him as he advanced. The bull was treated as his bull, and was attributed to private revenge. In many places the German people tore it down and trampled it underfoot, and at Erfurt the students threw the copies they obtained into the river. Several of the bishops refused to publish it. But grave danger threatened the reformer. If the mighty hand of the Emperor unites with that of the Pope, who can save the poor monk? For centuries the sentence of excommunication has been followed by death. What will Luther do? All eyes were turned towards him. While the bull was on its way he published his tract on "The Babylonian Captivity of the Church," closing it with these words: "I hear that new papal excommunications have been concocted against me. If it be so, this book may be considered as a part of my recantations. The rest will follow shortly in proof of my obedience, and the complete work will, by Christ's help, form such a whole as Rome has never yet seen or heard of."

On 3rd October the bull was published. Upon hearing of this Luther said, "I despise it, and attack it as impious, false, and in every respect worthy of Eck." A month later he issued his treatise "Against the Bull of Antichrist"; but a still more daring step was held in reserve. On the 17th November, he again appealed, in the presence of a notary and five witnesses, from the Pope to a General Christian Council hereafter to be held.

On the 10th December, a placard was fixed to the walls of the University of Wittemberg, inviting the professors and students to be present at nine o'clock the following morning at the east gate. A large number assembled. Luther led the way to the appointed spot. A fire was lighted, and as the flames rose high into the air he approached and cast the canonical law books, some writings of Eck's, and the Pope's bull into the fire, saying as he did so, "Since thou hast vexed the Holy One of the Lord, may everlasting fire vex and consume thee."

By this bold act he broke down the bridge of retreat; henceforth he must go onward or die. Great efforts were now made by the papal party to obtain from the Emperor an edict sentencing Luther to death. But Charles V. referred the papal nuncios to the Elector of Saxony.

The importance of gaining over the Elector to their side was fully estimated by Luther's enemies, and an interview with that prince was sought. "In your Highness are reposed all our hopes for the salvation of the Church and the Holy Roman Empire," pleaded Aleander the nuncio; and then he added with great vehemence, "Unless a remedy be speedily applied the empire is ruined. I require two things of you in the name of his Holiness: first, that you will burn Luther's writings; secondly, that you will inflict on him the punishment he deserves, or at least that you will deliver him to the Pope."

The Elector took time to reply to this violent speech. He was placed in a difficult position. He feared to offend the Pope, and he shrank from delivering up one whom he had long befriended. A youthful voice pleaded for the reformer. John Frederick, the Elector's nephew, then seventeen years of age, wrote to his uncle on Luther's behalf.

The Elector was just, and refused to give way to the wishes of the Pope. He replied to the nuncios, "Neither his imperial majesty nor any other person had shown that Luther's writings had been refuted, and that they deserved to be thrown into the fire," and he requested "that Doctor Luther should be furnished with a safe-conduct, so that he might appear before a tribunal of learned, pious, and impartial judges."

But while the agents of Rome were trying their utmost to destroy the reformer, Germany was overwhelming him with acclamations. Although the plague was raging in Wittemberg, new students arrived every day, and from four to six hundred disciples habitually sat at the feet of Luther and Melancthon. The two churches that belonged to the convent and the town were not large enough to hold the crowds who came to hear the reformer. Princes, nobles, and learned men from every quarter wrote him letters full of consolation and faith. But some of his friends grew timid, and seemed about to leave him. Staupitz was one of these. To him Luther wrote, " You exhort me to be humble, I exhort you to be firm."

> God will keep His own anointed,
>   Naught shall harm them, none condemn,
> All their trials are appointed,
>   All must work for good to them ;
> All shall help them
>   To their heavenly diadem.

CHAPTER XI.

The Diet of Worms.

"And ye shall be brought before governors and kings for my sake, for a testimony against them."—MATT. x. 18.

WE now come to the grandest scene in Luther's life—his appearance before the Diet of Worms.

As Nuremberg, where the Diet should have been held, was suffering from the plague, it was summoned to meet at Worms on the 6th January, 1521.

All the princes wished to be present, and as they journeyed along the roads leading to the city, the chief topic of conversation was the cause of the monk of Wittemberg. Important business connected with the empire was to be transacted; but the principal subject for discussion, it was understood, would be the Reformation.

In his desire to please both the Pope and the Elector, the Emperor requested Frederick to bring Luther with him to the Diet. This request perplexed the Elector, who feared that at any moment the alliance of the Pope might become necessary to

Charles V., and then the reformer would be sacrificed. Spalatin communicated the contents of the letter to Luther. His friends were alarmed, but he did not tremble. His health was very weak, but that did not matter. He looked upon the call as coming from God. "If I cannot go to Worms in good health," he wrote to the Elector, "I will be carried there weak as I am. If they desire to use violence against me, which is very probable, I place the matter in the Lord's hands. He still lives and reigns who preserved the three young men out of the burning fiery furnace. If He will not save me, my life is of very little consequence. You may expect anything from me except flight and recantation. Fly, I cannot, and still less retract."

Before this letter reached him Frederick had set out for Worms without the reformer.

The Diet was opened on the 28th January, 1521. The papal nuncios did not want Luther at Worms. What evils might not arise to the papacy from the presence of the monk, with his powerful eloquence! A second bull was therefore issued by the Pope; the former threatened Luther with excommunication, this pronounced the sentence against him and his adherents. Every nerve was strained and intrigues resorted to by the papal party, to prevail upon the Emperor to issue a stringent edict enforcing this bull; and Charles V. prepared one, which he laid before the assembled princes.

It was, however, necessary to gain over the Diet. Aleander undertook the task. For three hours he pleaded, with all the eloquence of which he was master; he even offered himself to be burned if only the monster Luther could be burned with him. "Fear not," he said; "in Luther's errors there is enough to burn a hundred thousand heretics. Let the axe be laid to the root of this poisonous tree."

The effect upon the assembly was great, but it quickly passed away. It was resolved that the reformer should appear before the Diet; and safe-conducts were eventually granted to him by the Emperor and by those princes through whose territories he would have to pass.

The summons to appear was handed to Luther by the imperial herald on the 24th March. Will he obey it?

The Elector wrote to his brother: "Doctor Martin has been summoned here, but I do not know whether he will come. I cannot augur any good from it."

But Luther has been called, and go he will!

On the 2nd April he took leave of his friends. Turning to Melancthon he said, "My dear brother, if I do not return, and should my enemies put me to death, continue to teach, and stand fast in the truth." Then, commending himself to God, he got into the car provided for him by the town council, and, amidst the prayers and tears of friends and citizens, he set out upon his perilous journey.

Preceded by the herald, carrying the imperial eagle, and accompanied by his friends Schurff, Amsdorff, and Suaven, he pressed onward. Gloomy fears filled the hearts of all whom he met. At

The Diet of Worms.

Naumburg, a priest held before him a portrait of Savonarola, who had been burnt a few years previously; and at Weimar his ears were greeted with the cries of the people as they watched the messenger posting up an edict which the Emperor had issued, commanding that his writings should be given up to the magistrates.

From Weimar, where he preached, he proceeded to Erfurt. As he was approaching that town he was received by a body of senators and distinguished friends, who escorted him within its walls. Passing onwards, and being now accompanied by Justus Jonas, a most powerful preacher, as well as by his other friends, he reached Eisenach, at which place he was taken seriously ill. A night's rest, however, restored him, and he was able on the following day to continue his journey.

As he went along, crowds of people flocked around him. They gazed with emotion upon the intrepid monk. "Ah!" said some, "there are so many bishops and cardinals at Worms, they will burn you as they did John Huss." Nothing daunted, he replied, "Though they should kindle a fire all the way from Worms to Wittemberg, the flames of which reached to heaven, I would walk through it, in the name of the Lord, and would appear before them."

On Sunday, 14th April, he entered into Frankfort, from which place he wrote to Spalatin desiring that a lodging might be prepared for him.

A plot was now devised by the papal party to draw him aside to Ebernburg until the safe-conduct expired; but through his firm determination to keep straight onward, it was foiled.

Spalatin, who was with the Elector at Worms, trembling for the result of the reformer's appearance in that city, sent a special messenger entreating him to beware of proceeding farther. To this messenger he answered, "Go and tell your master, that even should there be as many devils in Worms as tiles upon the house tops, still I would enter it!"

At length, on the morning of the 16th April, Luther saw the walls of the ancient city. All were anxiously expecting him. An escort, composed of young nobles, knights, and gentlemen, rode out to meet him. A great crowd was waiting at the gates of the city, and two thousand persons accompanied him through its streets.

The news of his arrival filled both the Emperor and the papal nuncios with alarm. Charles V. immediately summoned his council. "Luther is come," said he, "what must we do?" Rome gave an answer. She gave advice which had already been tried. Let your Imperial Majesty get rid of the man at once," said the Bishop of Palermo; "did not Sigismund cause John Huss to be burnt? We are not bound either to give or to observe the safe-conduct of a heretic." "No!" said Charles, "we must keep our promise."

On the next morning, Luther was summoned to appear at four o'clock in the afternoon before his Imperial Majesty and the States of the Empire. The hour approached. For a moment this intrepid soldier of Christ felt dismayed, as he thought of the august assembly before which he had to appear; but he pleaded with God, and strength was given. At four o'clock he followed the Imperial herald and the marshal of the empire to the Town Hall. Crowds thronged the streets, all the windows were occupied and the tops of the houses covered with spectators; the people quite blocked the way, and the herald, seeing the difficulty of advancing, led Luther through some private houses and gardens to the place where the Diet was sitting.

He stood before the door which was to admit him into the presence of his judges, and as he was about to pass through, a kindly hand tapped him on the shoulder, and the valiant old knight—the hero of many battles—George Freundsberg, said, " Poor monk, poor monk! thou art now going to make a nobler stand than I or any other captains have ever made in the fiercest of our battles. But if thy cause is just, and thou art sure of it, go forward in God's name, and fear nothing. God will not forsake thee!"

The doors were passed, and Luther stood in the presence of the Diet. Never had man appeared before a more imposing assembly. Seated upon the throne was Charles V.; surrounding him were the Archduke Ferdinand, six electors, dukes, margraves, archbishops and bishops, princes, the papal nuncios, and ambassadors—in all above two hundred; such was the court before which the reformer stood.

For a moment he was somewhat awed. One of

the princes, seeing this, whispered kindly, "Fear not them which kill the body, but are not able to kill the soul."

He approached and stood before the throne of the Emperor. Silence for a moment prevailed; and then the chancellor to the Archbishop of Treves, in a clear loud voice, said, "Martin Luther! his Sacred Majesty has cited you before his throne to require you to answer two questions: First, Do you acknowledge these books" — pointing to about twenty volumes placed on a table—"to have been written by you? Second, Are you prepared to retract these books and their contents; or do you persist in what you have advanced in them?"

After the titles of the books had been read, Luther made answer to the first question by stating that the books named were his; but as the second question concerned faith and the salvation of souls, he entreated that his Imperial Majesty would allow him time so that he might answer without offending against the Word of God.

As the reformer had spoken in a respectful manner and in a low tone of voice, many thought that he hesitated, and even that he was dismayed. Charles V., who had never taken his eyes off him, turned to one of his courtiers and said with disdain, "Certainly this man will never make a heretic of me."

Luther's request was granted on the condition that he made his reply on the following day, verbally, and not in writing.

The Imperial herald conducted him back to his hotel.

The early part of the following day was spent in earnest prayer and in reading the Scriptures. As the hour approached for him to appear again in the presence of the Diet, he drew near the Word of God, which lay open upon the table, and with deep emotion, placing his left hand upon the sacred volume and raising his right towards heaven, he swore to remain faithful to the Gospel, and freely to confess his faith, even should he seal his testimony with his blood.

At four o'clock the herald appeared to conduct him to the Diet. After waiting for two hours, surrounded by a dense crowd, which rocked backwards and forwards like the sea in a storm, he was admitted, and again stood before the throne of the Emperor, calm and confident.

The chancellor having asked for a reply, Luther, in a speech which lasted two hours, stated modestly, but with energy and firmness, in German, that he adhered to his former answer as to his being the author of the books attributed to him, and that as soon as it was proved by the writings of the prophets and apostles that he had erred, he would be the first to retract every error and cast his books into the fire; but that until he was convinced he was in error he could not retract. This speech he repeated in Latin.

When he had ceased speaking, the chancellor of Treves said indignantly, " You have not answered the question put to you. You are required to give a clear and precise answer; will you, or will you not retract?"

"Since your most Serene Majesty and your High Mightinesses require from me a clear, simple, and precise answer," replied Luther, "I will give you one, and it is this: I cannot submit my faith either to the Pope or to the Councils, because it is clear as the day that they have frequently erred and contradicted each other. Unless, therefore, I am convinced by the testimony of Scripture, or by the clearest reasoning —unless I am persuaded by means of the passages I have quoted,—and unless they thus render my conscience bound by the Word of God, I cannot, and I will not retract, for it is unsafe for a Christian to speak against his conscience." And looking round upon the assembly which held his life in its hands, he said: "Here I stand, I can do no other; may God help me! Amen!"

The assembly was motionless with amazement. The Emperor, recovering himself, exclaimed, "This monk speaks with an intrepid heart and unshaken courage."

As soon as the Diet had recovered from the impression produced, the chancellor said: "If you do not retract, the Emperor, and the States of the Empire, will consult what course to adopt against an incorrigible heretic."

Luther repeated: "May God be my helper; for I can retract nothing."

He then withdrew, but was soon called back again, and another effort was made to induce him to retract.

But firm as a rock he stood, while all the waves of human power dashed ineffectually against him. "I have no other reply to make than that which I have already made," was his final answer.

It was now night, and Luther was conducted back to his hotel. As he went along the streets, escorted by two officers, some friends exclaimed, "Are they taking him to prison?" "No," said Luther, "they are conducting me to my hotel."

Arrived at the hotel, the weary monk, surrounded by Spalatin and other friends, gave thanks to God. As they were conversing, a servant entered bearing a silver flagon full of Eimbeck beer.

"My master," said he, as he offered it to Luther, "invites you to refresh yourself with this draught."

"Who is the prince who so graciously remembers me?" inquired he.

It was the aged Duke Eric of Brunswick.

"His Highness tasted it before sending it to you," continued the servant.

Luther was affected by this kindness; and as, thirsty and tired, he poured out some of the beer, he said, "As this day Duke George has remembered me, so may our Lord Jesus Christ remember him in the hour of his last struggle."

The servant repeated the words to his master, and when dying Duke George remembered them.

Calling to a young page, he said, "Take the Bible and read to me." The page read those beautiful words of the Saviour, "Whosoever shall give you a cup of water to drink in my name, because ye belong to Christ, verily I say unto you, he shall not lose his reward." The dying prince was comforted.

The Elector was greatly delighted by the noble courage of the reformer, and he determined to protect him more openly in future.

The next day, 19th April, the Emperor ordered a message to be read to the Diet, which he had written in French with his own hand. In this he said: "A single monk, misled by his own folly, has risen against the faith of Christendom. To stay such impiety, I will sacrifice my kingdoms, my treasures, my friends, my body, my blood, my soul, and my life. I am about to dismiss the Augustine Luther, forbidding him to cause the least disorder among the people. I shall then proceed against him and his adherents as contumacious heretics, by excommunication, by interdict, and by every means calculated to destroy them."

Yet another attempt was made to get Luther to retract. This was undertaken in a kindly manner by the Archbishop of Treves, and by several princes who felt deeply interested in him; but he remained firm, and professed himself ready rather to lose his life than forsake the Word of God.

The Emperor was very indignant when he heard that this effort had proved useless, and exclaimed, "It is time to put an end to this business." He gave Luther twenty-one days, in which he was to return home, and forbade him to disturb the public peace on his road, either by preaching or writing.

Having taken leave of his friends, the reformer

quitted Worms, on Friday, the 26th April. Twenty gentlemen on horseback surrounded the car, and a large crowd of people accompanied him beyond the walls of the city.

Luther's account of the proceedings at Worms is very brief. He wrote to his friend Lucas Cranach— "I thought his Majesty would have assembled some fifty doctors at Worms to convict the monk outright. But not at all. 'Are these your books?' 'Yes!' 'Will you retract them?' '**No!**' 'Well, begone!' That is the whole history."

> Though numerous hosts of mighty foes,
> Though earth and hell my way oppose;
> He safely leads my soul along,
> His loving-kindness, oh, how strong!
>
> When troubles, like a gloomy cloud,
> Have gathered thick, and thunder'd loud;
> He near my soul has always stood,
> His loving-kindness, oh, how good!

CHAPTER XII.

The Wartburg.

"I will say of the Lord, He is my refuge and my fortress: my God; in Him will I trust."—Ps. xci. 2.

WHILE Luther was proceeding on his way to Wittemberg, the Emperor signed an edict in the Cathedral of Worms, in which, after stating that the reformer had rushed like a madman on our holy Church, he went on to say: "We have dismissed from our presence this Luther, whom all pious and sensible men count a madman, or one possessed by the devil; and we enjoin that, on the expiration of his safe-conduct, immediate recourse be had to effectual measures to check his furious rage." The edict further stated that no one was to harbour him, to give him food or drink, or to furnish him by word or deed with any kind of succour whatever, under pain of incurring the penalties due to high treason. His adherents were to be imprisoned, and their property was to be confiscated.

Meanwhile, he who was the subject of this terrible

condemnation was quietly journeying onward. He preached at Eisenach, where, as a boy, he had been kindly received by the good Ursula Cotta. He visited his aged grandmother at Mora, and now he is travelling along a road skirting the woods of Thuringia. Seated in a waggon, with his brother James and friend Amsdorff, he is passing through a hollow way near the deserted church of Glisbach. Suddenly a sound of horses' feet is heard, and five horsemen, armed and masked, rush upon the little party. James Luther flees. The driver tries to resist; but one of the assailants, with a terrible voice, bids him "Stop!" and throws him to the ground. A second seizes Amsdorff, and keeps him at a safe distance. The rest drag Luther from the waggon, and, throwing a military cloak over his shoulders, place him upon a horse. All five assailants now gallop off, carrying their captive along with them into the gloomy recesses of the forest.

The report spread rapidly that the brave monk had been carried off. Some rejoiced, but many were astonished and indignant. A cry of grief resounded through Germany—" Luther has fallen into the hands of his enemies."

To avoid being followed, the horsemen took first one direction and then another, until the poor monk was quite exhausted, and entreated for a few minutes' rest. He was allowed to dismount, and drank some water from a brook which still bears his name, As soon as it grew dark his guards took a new road; and just before midnight they reached the foot of a mountain. On the top was an old castle called the Wartburg, surrounded by dark forests. The weary horses slowly ascended the steep path, and Luther was admitted within the gates. He dismounted in the court, and one of the horsemen led him into a chamber, where he found a knight's uniform and a sword. He was dressed in these garments, and enjoined to let his hair and beard grow. In the Wartburg he went by the name of Knight George.

The preacher of Wittemberg was now severed from his flock; the bold servant of the Most High, who feared not the face of man, was now a prisoner in a gloomy fortress. Was he in the hands of friends or foes?

Various reports were circulated. "Luther's body has been seen pierced through and through," reached the ears of his friends. "Alas!" said they, "we shall never see the noble-minded man again." At Wittemberg the grief was very great.

Suddenly startling news reached that town: "Luther is alive!" "Our beloved father lives!" exclaimed Melancthon, "take courage and be firm."

The news was indeed true. Luther was alive, but a captive. The Elector, seeing the fearful danger which surrounded the reformer, had planned his capture, so that he might be kept in safety from his foes.

The Reformation progressed, and, notwithstanding the edict of the Emperor, Luther's writings were read more and more.

While in the Wartburg, Luther was not idle. He wrote letters to his friends, dating them from the "Isle of Patmos," comparing his prison to the island to which the apostle John was banished. He secretly issued many tracts, and translated the New Testament into German. He also took great pains to improve his knowledge of both Greek and Hebrew, so that he might render his intended version of the Scriptures more complete. "Scripture without any comment," said he, "is the sun whence all teachers receive their light."

The solitary life now led by Luther did not suit him. He became weak and ill. His mind was depressed. Seated alone on the ramparts of the Wartburg, he remained whole days lost in deep meditation. He longed to be with his beloved people at Wittemberg, and once again contending for the truth against its many foes. Strange imaginations became to him living realities, and the enemy of mankind— Satan—appeared to assume a visible form. On one occasion, while engaged in translating the New Testament, he fancied that he beheld the prince of darkness prowling round him like a lion about to spring upon its prey. Alarmed and vexed, he snatched up his inkstand and flung it at the head of his enemy.

Day by day the restraint imposed upon him became more and more unendurable.

Tidings also reached him from Wittemberg, which enabling him sometimes to rejoice, at others caused him profound sorrow and anxiety. The Reformation was progressing, but the zeal of some of its supporters exceeded their discretion. While Luther rejoiced to hear that the mass had been declared to be unscriptural, and that thirteen monks had been led, through the influence of the Word of God, to leave their cloister, he felt sad and indignant when he heard that, in his beloved town, the churches were being broken into, priests insulted, books carried off, and images taken away and burned.

Another source of disquiet was occasioned by false prophets who came from Zwickau. They declared that they had received direct revelations from God; they cast the Bible aside, and despised learning. Many were led away, the University became disorganised, and the work of the Reformation was imperilled. In this hour of danger there was a general cry for Luther; he was the only one who could bring order out of this chaos.

At the end of November he had paid a secret visit to Wittemberg, and now he resolved to brave all the dangers that beset him and to leave his retreat. The Elector was averse to him doing so, but he could no longer remain inactive amidst the scenes which were taking place.

On the 3rd March, 1522, he bade farewell to the Wartburg, and set out for Wittemberg. When near Jena he was overtaken by a dreadful thunderstorm, and sought shelter at an inn called the Black Bear. Two young Swiss students were also passing onwards towards Wittemberg, and stopped at the same inn. Seated at a table, intently reading a book, was a knight who politely invited them to come and sit at his table, also offering them refreshment. Encouraged by his kindness, they said, " Sir, could you inform us where Martin Luther is at present?"

"I know for certain," answered the knight, "that he is not at Wittemberg, but he will be there shortly."

"If God spare our lives," said one of the young men, "we will not return home without having seen and heard Dr. Luther, for it is on his account that we have undertaken this long journey."

After supper the stranger knight shook hands with the students, and said, "When you reach Wittemberg salute Dr. Schurff from me."

"Most willingly," they replied; "but whose name shall we give?"

"Tell him simply," said the knight, "that he that is to come salutes you."

The knight was Luther, who continued his journey until he came to the little town of Borne, near Leipsic, from which place he wrote to the Elector, informing him of his intention to return to Wittemberg. In this letter he entreated his prince not to protect him, as no sword could further the Word of God. "You must offer no resistance if men desire to seize or kill me," he wrote, "for no one should resist dominions except He who has established them."

> Press forward, and fear not; though trials be near,
> The Lord is our refuge,—whom, then, shall we fear?
> His staff is our comfort, our safeguard His rod;
> Then let us be steadfast, and trust in our God.

CHAPTER XIII.

Return to Wittemberg.

"The Lord is my light and my salvation; whom shall I fear the Lord is the strength of my life; of whom shall I be afraid?
—Ps. xxvii. 1.

LUTHER entered Wittemberg again on Friday, 7th March. Doctors, students and people, all alike rejoiced.

On the Sunday he preached, and crowds flocked to the parish church to hear their much-loved pastor again. Very gently he dealt with his flock,—he called them "his own sheep,"—telling them that "violence can never propagate the Gospel; that must be done by the Word of God alone."

All were delighted. Schurff wrote to the Elector, "Oh, what joy has Dr. Martin's return diffused among us! His words through Divine mercy are every day bringing back our poor misguided people into the way of truth. It is clear that the Spirit of God is in him, and that by His special providence he returned to Wittemberg."

The tumult subsided, and quiet reigned. Liberty of conscience was established. Luther continued to reside in the convent, and to wear his monk's dress, but every one was free to do otherwise. The rule was laid down that nothing should be rejected except it were in opposition to the Holy Scriptures.

Tranquillity being restored, Luther sought Melancthon's assistance in finally revising his translation of the New Testament. The printing was carried on with great zeal. Three presses were employed, and 10,000 sheets printed daily.

On the 21st September, 1522, the first edition appeared. In a short time the whole of the 3000 copies issued were sold. A second edition followed in December.

In vain the Pope and princes burnt the Scriptures and forbade their circulation. The demand increased, and by the close of 1533 fifty-eight editions had been printed. Duke George said: " Even after I had prohibited the sale, many thousand copies were sold and read in my States."

The New Testament being finished, Luther commenced and carried on a translation of the Old Testament. Henry VIII., the King of England, had Luther's writings burnt, and wrote a book against the reformer, in which he called him a wolf and a viper. This so pleased the Pope that he conferred upon Henry the title of " Defender of the Faith,"— a title still borne by the kings and queens of England.

Leo X. died while Luther was in the Wartburg, and the new Pope was named Adrian VI.

But burning books could not stay the progress of the truth. Monks continued to leave their cells, and became preachers, colporteurs, or engaged in daily toil. The colporteurs travelled throughout Germany, selling Bibles and tracts to the people ; and preachers in the open air proclaimed the glad tidings of salvation.

Bitter persecutions now commenced. Duke George imprisoned the monks and priests who followed Luther. At Brussels, the first martyrs of the Reformation laid down their lives. Three young monks, named Henry Voes, John Esch, and Lambert Thorn, were led in chains to that city. When asked whether they would retract, they replied, " No ; we will retract nothing; we will not disown God's Word; we will rather die for the faith." Esch and Voes were burnt; and Lambert, who was terrified at the prospect of death, was taken back to prison; but soon he boldly confessed his faith, and died like his brethren.

Luther felt deeply for these noble young men, and composed the following verses in commemoration of their death :—

> " No, no ! their ashes shall not die !
> But, borne to every land,
> Where'er their sainted dust shall fall,
> Up springs a holy band.
>
> " Though Satan by his might may kill,
> And stop their powerful voice,
> They triumph o'er him in their death,
> And still in Christ rejoice."

In July, 1523, Adrian VI. died, and Clement VII. was elected Pope.

Many of the German princes now embraced the cause of the Reformation, amongst whom was Philip, the Landgrave of Hesse, who said: "Rather would I sacrifice my body, my life, my estates, and my subjects, than the Word of God." These princes favoured the preaching of the Gospel in their States, and boldly opposed the efforts of the papal party. The partisans of Rome became more and more enraged against the truth, and two rival camps began to be formed in the empire.

Dreadful scenes were now witnessed in Germany. The peasants, who for ages had been cruelly oppressed, had risen against the nobles. In vain Luther had written to them from the Wartburg, saying: "Rebellion never obtains for us the benefits we seek, and God condemns it. The devil is striving to excite to rebellion those who embrace the Gospel, in order to cover it with reproach; but those who have rightly understood my doctrine do not revolt." Despite his warning, the peasants rose, and fearful cruelties were committed. No mercy was shown, and day by day things grew more alarming. At length, two decisive battles were fought on one day, 15th May, 1525, and the insurrection was subdued. Upwards of fifty thousand perished.

Luther struggled hard against this rebellion; he prayed, he wrote, and, while the disturbances were still at their height, he travelled through the country calming men's minds and bringing them into subjection to the Word of God. None of the Elector's subjects rebelled.

The aged and pious Elector, the friend of Luther and the Reformation, expired on the 5th May, 1524. Just before his death he destroyed a will in which he had commended his soul to the Virgin Mary, and dictated another, in which he cast himself entirely upon the merits of Jesus Christ.

Frederick was succeeded by his brother John, who was a firm friend of the Reformation.

On the 13th of June, 1525, Luther married Catherine Bora. The wedding took place in the house of his friend, Amsdorff.

In the convent of Nimptsch, near Grimma, in Saxony, dwelt, in the year 1523, nine nuns, who were diligent in reading the Scriptures. Seeing that they had made a mistake in trying to serve God by shutting themselves out from the world, they wrote to their parents, saying, "The salvation of our souls will not permit us to remain any longer in a cloister. Their parents would not receive them, and, feeling in their own consciences that they ought not to remain, they left the nunnery in two waggons which friends had provided, and, knowing that they would find a friend in Luther, stopped at the gate of his monastery at Wittemberg. "This is not my doing," said he, as he received them, and rejoiced at their escape.

Several persons offered to receive the nuns into their houses, and Catherine Bora, who was one of them, found a home with the family of the burgomaster of Wittemberg.

At that time Luther had no intention of marrying, and recommended Catherine as a wife to two of his friends; but his father urged him to do so, and, after much serious thought, he said, "I am determined to bear witness to the Gospel, not by my words alone, but by my actions. I'll content my father, and marry Catherine." At the time of his marriage he was living alone in the convent at Wittemberg, and had laid aside the dress and name of a monk.

John, the Elector of Saxony, made the convent a present to Luther and his wife for a dwelling-house.

He was very happy in his marriage. "His dear and amiable Kertha," as he called Catherine, made him a good wife. She loved him much; and when dejected, she would console him by repeating passages of Scripture; she also worked his portrait in embroidery.

About a year after their marriage they had a son, whom they called John, and the next year a daughter, who was named Magdalen. In all they had six children. The old convent became a joyous home, and often might Luther and his Kertha have been seen sitting in the window, overlooking their beautiful garden, singing together sweet songs of praise. He was very fond of music.

But a dark cloud rested upon the bright and happy household. When fourteen years old, Magdalen became very ill, and died. Luther was much afflicted. Speaking of her, he said, "I love her well; but oh, my God, if it be Thy will to take her home, I must resign myself to Thee." When she was very near death, her father read to her from Isa. xxvi., and, falling upon his knees at her bedside, he wept bitterly, and entreated God to save her. She expired in his arms, in the presence of her mother. He often exclaimed, "God's will be done! My daughter has still a Father in heaven."

Philip Melancthon comforted his friend in this hour of sorrow.

> I've lost the child I held so dear,
> Nor can I check the flowing tear:
> But when I view Thy mercy-seat,
> My meditation shall be sweet.
>
> 'Tis true I weep, but thou hast smiled;
> Safe in Thy arms faith sees my child;
> I flee to Thee, my loved retreat,
> And meditation shall be sweet.

CHAPTER XIV.

Closing Scenes.

"Be thou faithful unto death, and I will give thee a crown of life."—Rev. ii. 10.

EIGHT years have passed away since Luther stood before the Diet of Worms, and another Diet was about to meet in the city of Spires.

The Reformation has continued to spread, and now not only the Elector and the young Landgrave of Hesse are faithful to its cause, but other princes, and thousands of the people, hold the truth dear to their hearts.

The papal party have made great efforts to get the Edict of Worms, against Luther and his associates, enforced; but through the fearless courage of the reforming princes their plans have been foiled, and it has been decided instead, that until a General Council meets, the Gospel alone shall be preached.

The Diet of Spires was opened on 29th June, 1526. Ferdinand, King of Bohemia, and brother of the Emperor, presided. The friends of the Gospel were outnumbered by the partisans of Rome, but their courage was unshaken. They opened the halls of their palaces for preaching the Word of God, and thousands congregated to hear the truth.

The Emperor had furnished Ferdinand with a decree, three months before, requiring that the "Church customs should be everywhere observed, and that the Edict of Worms should be confirmed." This decree was laid before the assembled princes, when many declared it was quite beyond their power to enforce it, and, although published, it was not carried into effect. Great fears were entertained that persecution was about to recommence; but just as the Pope and the Emperor seemed on the point of uniting to crush the Reformation, they quarrelled, and the forces ready to march against Germany were turned aside to Rome, which city was sacked amidst fearful carnage in May, 1527.

The Edict of Worms was suspended, and a season of rest ensued. Each State was allowed to act in religious matters as it thought right, giving account to God and the Emperor alone.

During this peaceful interval Luther, Melancthon, Spalatin, and another named Thuring, went throughout the country visiting the churches, teaching, admonishing, establishing new schools, and instructing the teachers.

In 1529, Luther issued his Catechism, which, next to his translation of the Bible, was his most useful work. In 1530, he wrote to the Elector—" Our youth now grow up so well instructed in the Scriptures and catechism, it does my heart good to see and hear them. Young boys and little maidens learn to believe and understand more of God and Christ than was formerly known in our cloisters and schools."

Peace having been concluded between the Pope and the Emperor, the Diet reassembled in March, 1529. A resolution was passed, by twenty votes against fourteen, by which the power granted three years ago to each State to regulate its own religious affairs was revoked, and all changes in the public religion were declared to be unlawful until the decision of the General Council should be known. This prevented the Reformation from being extended.

"Let us reject this decree," said the Lutheran princes; "in matters of conscience the majority have no power."

On the 18th April, Ferdinand appeared in the Diet, thanked the Romanists for their fidelity, said that the resolution, having been passed by a majority, would become an Imperial edict, and told the Elector and his friends that their part was submission. They retired to consult together, but Ferdinand would not wait. All entreaties were useless. "I have received an order from His Imperial Majesty," he said. "I have executed it. All is over."

But all was not over. The reforming princes drew up a formal protest, or declaration of their opinions, in which they appealed from the Diet to the Word of God, and from the Emperor Charles to Jesus Christ, the King of kings and Lord of lords. This protest they read before the Diet, and sent a copy to Ferdinand, who refused to accept it.

From that day the name Protestant has been given to all those who hold the truth in opposition to the Church of Rome.

The Protest of Spires was followed in 1530 by the Confession of Augsburg, and, after a season of warlike preparation and great anxiety, peace was concluded between the Emperor and the Protestants in 1532, when Germany enjoyed a season of quietness for several years.

We hasten on to the closing scenes of the reformer's life. In 1529, the discussion at Marburg between Luther and Zwingle—the Swiss reformer—was held, upon the presence of Christ's body in the Sacrament of the Lord's Supper, and soon afterwards, feeling the need of rest, he requested permission to retire into the country. The Elector preferred that he should remain at Wittemberg, and in that town he resided until a few weeks before his death.

In 1527 he was attacked by severe illness, and his life was despaired of. Thinking then that his end was near, he took leave of his wife and his little son; but he was not as yet destined to die. From this time, however, he was frequently subject to painful disease, which affected his head, and, towards the close, impaired his sight. But notwithstanding his increasing infirmities, he undertook a journey, in the winter of 1546, from Wittemberg to Eisleben, in the hope of settling a dispute which had arisen between the Dukes of Mansfeld and their subjects.

He set out on the 23rd of January, attended by his three sons. He reached Halle, but was so weak that his friend, Doctor Jonas, accompanied him for the rest of the journey. At Eisleben he was much worse, yet he preached four times, administered the Lord's Supper twice, and ordained two ministers. Till the 16th of February he attended all the meetings held for the purpose of arranging the dispute, and said, " If I can but succeed in restoring harmony amongst my dear princes and their subjects, I will cheerfully return home and lay me down in the grave."

On the 17th his illness increased. He spoke often of death and eternity, and prayed much. At night he complained of great oppression on his chest, and, feeling death approaching, he prayed, saying, " I beseech Thee, my Lord Jesus Christ, receive my soul. O Heavenly Father, though I be snatched out of this life, yet know I assuredly that I shall dwell with Thee for ever."

Then he exclaimed three times, " Father, into Thy hands I commit my spirit."

Doctor Jonas, said, " Venerable father, do you die firm in the faith you have taught ? " He distinctly answered, " Yes."

Between two and three o'clock in the morning of 18th February, 1546, he ceased to breathe. He had gone to be with that Saviour whom he loved so well.

His body was brought back to Wittemberg, and buried in the Church of All Saints. Dukes and nobles followed him to the grave.

Besides his widow, Catherine, he left behind him three sons and two daughters.

More than three hundred years have passed since Luther died, but he being dead yet speaketh. His firm adherence to the truth, his dauntless courage, his prayerful spirit and solemn regard for Divine things, his faith in God, and his zeal in pursuing that which was right, speak to us from afar; and his memory will ever be venerated by those whose delight is in the law of the Lord, and whose aim it is to do His will.

In 1821, William III., King of Prussia, ordered a monument to be erected to Luther in the market-square of Wittemberg, and in 1868 a magnificent memorial was inaugurated in the city of Worms; but Luther's best memorial exists in the noble work which he was called to accomplish, in the faithful translation of the Scriptures which he gave to Germany, in his beautiful hymns, and in the loving gratitude of tens of thousands of Christian hearts.

>   Servant of God, well done!
>   Rest from thy loved employ;
>   The battle o'er, the victory won,
>   Receive thy crown with joy.

PRINTED AND MANUFACTURED IN SCOTLAND